The Restored Workplace

How Healing Broken Relationships Unlocks Destiny and Profit

Marla A. McCarthy

Real Life Series Publishing

ISBN: 979-8-9989754-9-3
Library of Congress Control Number: 2025916864

First Printing 2025

Inquires should be addressed to:
The Real Life Series Publishing Co., LLC
rlspublishing@gmail.com

Dedication

This book is for every courageous leader, visionary, and team member committed to healing broken relationships and unlocking the extraordinary potential in every individual.

You have chosen the path less traveled, understanding that true greatness in business comes from healed hearts, restored trust, and renewed purpose.

Your daily dedication transforms lives, rebuilds hope, and ignites destinies, creating workplaces that thrive not just financially, but in the richness of genuine human connection.

May the pages of this book empower and encourage you as you lead boldly, communicate compassionately, and foster environments where every person feels valued, honored, and inspired to do their greatest work.

Together, let's spark a global movement of workplace restoration, leaving a legacy of healing, unity, success, fulfillment of purpose, and lasting prosperity.

Table of Contents

197

INTRODUCTION

Healing Workplaces, Unlocking Destiny

Have you ever walked into a workplace and felt the *heaviness* in the air, even before a single word was spoken? Have you ever carried the silent burden of betrayal, broken trust, or unresolved conflict with a coworker, feeling it slowly drain your energy, stifle your creativity, and dim your sense of purpose?

Or perhaps you've looked around at your team or organization and thought, "We could be so much more, if only we could get past all this division." If any of that feels familiar, I wrote this book for you.

The Restored Workplace is not just another book about workplace culture. It is a clarion call to heal what has been broken, build what's been missing, and unlock the destinies trapped beneath strained relationships, missed opportunities, and exhausted teams.

This is not about surface-level fixes or temporary solutions. It's about transforming the foundation of how we work together: heart to heart, leader to team member, person to person. Because when people heal, workplaces heal. When workplaces heal, destinies are unlocked. And when destinies are unlocked, the world changes.

When you finish reading *The Restored Workplace*, you will have the tools and wisdom to heal broken relationships even when trust has been deeply wounded. You will learn how to communicate with courageous clarity, even during the most challenging conversations, and rebuild trust where it has been lost. You will know how to create cultures of psychological safety, where people feel valued, heard, and empowered to give their very best.

Whether you are a manager, team leader, entrepreneur, ministry leader, or a committed team member, you will be equipped with the emotional intelligence needed to recognize and resolve hidden conflicts, establish boundaries that create respect instead of resentment, and walk in forgiveness that liberates not only others, but also your own heart.

You will learn how to build workplaces where people thrive, not just survive; and align your daily work with your higher purpose and God-given destiny, allowing your impact to ripple far beyond the walls of your organization.

Within these pages, you will also find *real* answers to the everyday challenges that are silently stealing potential from workplaces everywhere: miscommunication, misunderstandings, gossip, low morale, high turnover, broken trust, hidden tension, unresolved hurt, competitive division, and a devastating lack of belonging and unity.

If you have ever witnessed stalled growth, declining innovation, or lost profitability, you will discover that relational dysfunction, not a lack of talent or strategy, is often the true culprit. And you will find clear, actionable pathways to restoration.

Why am I so passionate about this? Because I have lived it. As a wife of over 25 years, a mother of seven exceptional children, and a life and empowerment coach to women and leaders, I have seen firsthand that the health of our relationships determines the health of our lives.

This is not just about workplace conflict. It's about dreams dying quietly behind office doors. It's about men and women carrying unseen wounds from their workplaces into their homes, marriages, families, and communities. It's about vibrant, God-given talents and abilities being buried under disappointment, bitterness, and burnout, all because no one taught us how to heal, communicate with grace and courage, or to lead with love and strength simultaneously.

I have seen how broken workplaces create broken people and, gloriously, how healed workplaces create world changers.

My passion is simple, but it burns fiercely in my heart: **I want to see you win.** I want to see you rise in your career, business, workplace relationships, family, and everyday life. I want to see you walk boldly into the purpose and destiny God designed uniquely for you. Because when you win, the world wins. When you heal, generations are changed. And when you step fully into your restored destiny, you give silent but powerful permission for others to do the same.

This book is an invitation to see your workplace through a new lens: one shaped by grace, wisdom, and purpose. Blending timeless biblical truths with practical coaching strategies, these pages will guide you toward healthier relationships, stronger communication, and a more profound sense of meaning in your daily work. You'll learn how to navigate conflict with courage and compassion, rebuild trust, and cultivate a culture rooted in integrity, collaboration, and renewed vision. More than just tools for success, this journey offers transformation from the inside out, as your mind, heart, and spirit are gently renewed.

And do not be conformed to this world {any longer with its superficial values and customs}, but be transformed and progressively changed {as you mature spiritually} by the renewing of your mind {focusing on godly values and ethical attitudes}, so that you may prove {for yourselves} what the will of God is, that which is good and acceptable and perfect {in His plan and purpose for you}.
— Romans 12:2, AMP

This is the sacred journey of the Restorer. And make no mistake: you were born for this. You are not here by accident. You are not reading these words by coincidence. God Himself is inviting you into a movement of courageous men and women who believe that how we work together matters just as much as the work we do.

A movement of Restorers who will heal workplaces and, through them, help heal the world. The work ahead of us is great, but the reward is even greater.

Healing, unity, profit, purpose, and destiny. It all starts right here. Right now. Will you answer the call?

Welcome to *The Restored Workplace*. Let's begin the journey together.

Why The World Needs A Restored Workplace

The brokenness we see in workplaces today isn't just unfortunate; it's an epidemic. It's a silent, corrosive force draining human potential, fueling division, crushing creativity, and quietly suffocating the destinies of individuals, families, organizations, and even entire communities. The tragedy is that it happens so gradually that many have accepted dysfunction, mistrust, and disconnection as simply "the way things are."

We see the evidence all around us. According to a 2023 Gallup report, only 23% of employees worldwide feel engaged at work, meaning nearly eight out of ten workers are either quietly disengaged or actively resentful. In other words, the vast majority of people spend the majority of their waking hours in environments where they feel undervalued, unseen, or disconnected from any real sense of purpose.

Conflict, too, remains a devastating, silent thief. A major global study found that U.S. companies lose an estimated $359 billion annually to the effects of workplace conflict, including lost productivity, absenteeism, turnover, and legal costs. Meanwhile, the World Health Organization has officially classified burnout as a *syndrome,* a sobering acknowledgment that unchecked workplace stress is causing emotional and physical harm at historic levels.

But this is not just about the bottom line. It's about souls. The essence of the being of persons, encompassing their mind, will, emotions, and personality, the part of people that gives life to their being, is being harmed *in the workplace.*

It's about people walking away from their jobs, and often from their dreams, emotionally wounded, spiritually depleted, and relationally isolated. It's about potential lying dormant. Gifts unopened. Dreams quietly dying in the midst of a 9-to-5, buried under resentment, fear, and frustration. God never intended it to be this way.

God's Original Design for Workplaces

From the very beginning, work was never intended to be a burden. In the Garden of Eden, God placed Adam not to struggle, but to partner with Him 'to work it and take care of it' (Genesis 2:15). Work was meant to be a life-giving expression of creativity, stewardship, and shared purpose, a sacred opportunity to bring beauty, order, and meaning into the world.

As Scripture says, 'So the Lord God took the man [He had made] and settled him in the Garden of Eden to cultivate and keep it' (Genesis 2:15, AMP). This original design reflects God's heart for our work: that it would be fulfilling, collaborative, and connected to something greater than ourselves.

But as we know, the human story took a turn. When sin entered the world, a disconnect from God's ways, whether through thought, word, or action, the nature of work underwent a shift. What was once joyful became marked by competition, mistrust, and toil (Genesis 3:17–19). Instead of working with one another, we often find ourselves working against each other.

Still, that isn't where the story ends. In the midst of brokenness, Christ came not only to heal individual hearts but to restore how we live, lead, and work together. Scripture

provides us with timeless blueprints for building trust, resolving conflict, and cultivating communities where people
can flourish, mentally, emotionally, and spiritually.

*Do nothing from selfishness or empty conceit {through factional mo-
tives, or strife}, but with {an attitude of} humility {being neither
arrogant nor self-righteous}, regard others as more important than
yourselves. — Philippians 2:3, AMP*

*Let everything you do be done in love {motivated and inspired by
God's love for us}. — 1 Corinthians 16:14, AMP*

*If a house is divided against itself, that house cannot stand.
— Mark 3:25, NIV*

*Plans fail for lack of counsel, but with many advisers they succeed.
— Proverbs 15:22, NIV*

The truths we find in Scripture aren't just inspirational
sayings; they are time-tested principles for restoring dignity, nurturing unity, and creating a culture where people
can truly thrive. These timeless values apply not only in our
homes and communities but just as powerfully in our workplaces.

When we choose to lead with love, show respect, listen
with intention, and extend forgiveness instead of holding on
to offense, something begins to shift. We don't just improve
our relationships with colleagues, we begin to reflect the
kind of character that brings lasting change. In doing so, we
become faithful stewards of the influence and opportunities
God has entrusted to us, right where we've been planted.

Why Broken Workplaces Are So Costly

Broken relationships don't just hurt feelings, they devastate organizations and many times also harm the families of employees within those organizations. When mistrust, gossip, resentment, and unresolved conflict are allowed to fester in workplaces:

- Innovation slows because people are afraid to risk or share ideas.
- Productivity plummets because energy is spent navigating tension, not fulfilling assignments.
- Creativity withers under the weight of fear and judgment.
- Employee retention drops because no one wants to stay where they feel unsafe or unseen.
- Profits shrink because disconnection *always* leads to dysfunction.

The impact of a broken workplace rarely stays contained within office walls. The stress, tension, and toxicity often follow people home, affecting marriages, parenting, friendships, and even health. When leaders are hurting, that pain can unintentionally shape the environments around them, creating a ripple effect that reaches far beyond the workplace.

When workplaces are fractured, so much potential is left unrealized. Talents are overlooked. Voices grow quiet. The greater purpose God has placed within people can feel delayed or even forgotten. That's why healing our work environments isn't just a noble goal; it's part of a deeper calling. Restoring the workplace is one of the ways we help restore lives, communities, and Kingdom impact.

What a Restored Workplace Could Look Like

What if your workplace became a place of peace, purpose, and shared growth?

Imagine, really imagine, a work environment where:

- People listen with intention and respond with patience (James 1:19).
- Conflicts are handled directly, yet gently, with love at the center (Matthew 18:15).
- Leaders serve with humility, rather than seeking control (Luke 22:26).
- Team members genuinely honor and celebrate each other's strengths (Romans 12:10).
- Forgiveness isn't withheld, and past wounds aren't carried like armor (Colossians 3:13).
- Decisions are guided by integrity, compassion, and a sense of justice (Micah 6:8).

Picture stepping into that kind of atmosphere, not needing to spiritually brace yourself just to get through the day (Ephesians 6:11–18), but arriving as your whole, God-created self.

Your gifts. Your voice. Your compassion. Your creativity. All are welcomed and valued. This isn't wishful thinking. It's not a fantasy. It's what *restoration* makes possible.

And the starting point isn't a new HR policy or the next team-building event. It begins in the heart. It begins with lives quietly but powerfully transformed by Christ, with minds renewed through His Word, and with people (people like you) who are willing to build something better, together.

A Coaching Moment: Reflect and Prepare

I invite you to take a moment right now and reflect:

1. Where have I seen brokenness steal life and joy from a workplace I've been part of?
2. Where have I been personally wounded?
3. Or where might I have unknowingly contributed to someone else's hurt?
4. What would it look like for me to be *a Restorer* in my current workplace?

Restoration does not require a title. It doesn't require permission from your HR department or a leadership badge. It only requires one willing heart and *leading by example.*

A heart that says: "God, use me. Heal through me. Restore through me." You have been placed in your position, your team, your circle of influence, for such a time as this.

Closing Thought: Restoration Is Possible, and Powerful

The world desperately needs restored workplaces, not just because brokenness is exhausting and expensive, but because *healing is life-giving, destiny-shaping, and world-changing.*

When workplaces are restored, people flourish, families are strengthened, and communities heal. An inner transformation, a change of heart and mind that allows God to work in us, begins to cause our lives and businesses to thrive in the way God intended, and God's Kingdom advances.

You don't need to wait. You don't need to be perfect. You don't even need a leadership title. You simply need a willing spirit, a renewed mind, a loving spirit, and the courage to take the first step as a Restorer. The world is waiting. The workplace is ready. The restoration begins now. And it begins with you.

.

PERSONAL STORY

Personal Story: The Revelation That Set This Book and This Movement in Motion

I never set out to write a book about restoring workplaces. I simply set out to live a life of purpose, love my family well, build a legacy of faith, and help women discover the fullness of who God created them to be.

As a wife of over twenty-five years, a mother of seven beautiful children, six sons and one daughter, and a life and empowerment coach to women, my journey has been deeply rooted in navigating the delicate tension between professional dreams and personal responsibilities. Every season of life taught me something new about juggling calling and commitment, ambition and family, dreams and diapers, leadership and love.

And somewhere along the way, as I walked alongside numerous women, coaching them through career milestones, life transitions, heartbreaks, and breakthroughs, I began to notice a painful, recurring pattern. So many women, gifted, capable, hard-working women, were struggling inside workplaces that were never designed with their full humanity and the fulfillment of their full potential in mind.

Workplaces that demanded endless availability but offered little flexibility. Workplaces that celebrated productivity but turned a blind eye to the personal cost it took to maintain it. Workplaces that valued titles and profit over people's families, marriages, health, children, faith, and souls.

I heard story after story. Women who hid their pregnancies out of fear that they would lose opportunities. Women burning themselves out, believing that if they didn't "do it all," they'd be seen as less than: less committed, less valuable, less capable.

Mothers quietly sacrificing milestones, memories, and moments because their jobs didn't recognize the fullness of who they were, not just employees, but daughters, sisters, nurturers, caretakers, and leaders in their homes and communities.

However, the heartbreak wasn't limited to their stories. Men were silently carrying their own weight of invisible expectations. Many had been conditioned from a young age to perform without showing emotion, to succeed without admitting struggle, to lead without vulnerability or support.

Some were fathers missing dinners and bedtime routines, not because they didn't care, but because they felt they had no choice. Some were husbands carrying the pressure of provision alone, with no space to say, "I'm overwhelmed." Some were leaders at work, expected to have all the answers, even as they battled anxiety, burnout, or a quiet sense of disconnection.

In both men and women, I saw this common thread: people stretched thin, carrying burdens they were never meant to bear alone. People trying to live and lead with excellence, but without the emotional, spiritual, or relational support that fuels sustainability.

When our workplaces ignore the full humanity of the people within them, everyone suffers. However, when we begin to honor the whole person, regardless of gender, role, or position, we create the space for healing, wholeness, and restoration.

So the revelation became clear: It's not the people who

are broken. *It's the way we are building our workplaces that is broken.* Somewhere along the way, we lost the truth that workplace is meant to serve people, not enslave them. Leadership is meant to lift people higher, not grind them down. Workplaces are meant to be environments where purpose thrives, not where souls are slowly drained.

Like our homes and our churches, workplaces are sacred spaces where we spend so many hours of our lives. They should be places of safety, belonging, growth, and honor where a person's gifts, struggles, dreams, and responsibilities are not liabilities to be hidden, but treasures to be honored and contributing factors to the success of each business and organization.

The Deeper Challenges Women Face

In coaching women across industries, I witnessed consistent struggles that cannot and must not be ignored: Many women are expected to work as if they have no children, and parent as if they have no jobs. This double standard leads to exhaustion, guilt, and eventual burnout.

Women often perform invisible labor at work, nurturing team morale, resolving conflict, and maintaining emotional safety, without recognition or reward. Flexibility is still seen as a privilege, not a standard, making it difficult for women (and men) to meet the very real needs of family life without being professionally penalized.

Leadership barriers persist, even today, with glass ceilings and unconscious biases limiting the growth of gifted, driven women across industries. Many women feel isolated in workplaces that fail to prioritize mentorship, emotional support, and holistic development.

Perhaps the most heartbreaking reality is that women are often forced to choose between their God-given dreams and their families, silently questioning whether the workplace values their worth as fully as God does.

The Solutions: God's Blueprint for Workplaces That Heal and Thrive

A restored workplace does not demand people erase parts of themselves to succeed.

It honors the whole person: their gifts, faith, families, and emotional and mental well-being as valuable contributions, not burdens.

Imagine a workplace where flexibility is not a begrudging exception but a joyful standard of trust.

Where leadership means *true service:* lifting, equipping, and protecting the team, not exploiting them for personal gain. Where collaboration replaces toxic competition, and strengths are celebrated instead of vulnerabilities being weaponized. Where work-life integration is honored, recognizing that when people are healthy at home, they are stronger at work.

Where mental health and emotional wellness are prioritized as essential parts of a thriving, creative, purpose-driven organization. Where biblical, wisdom-filled values: humility, honor, compassion, forgiveness, stewardship, are not just posters on a wall but living realities shaping every interaction and every decision.

This isn't just a "nice idea." It's God's blueprint. It is the path to workplaces that prosper ethically, produce profitably, and lead people into their destinies.

Why This Book and This Movement Had to Be Born

One day, *our time on this earth will come to an end.* And when it does, few of us will wish we had logged more hours, sat through more meetings, or climbed one more rung on the corporate ladder.

But we will carry the weight of how we treated people. We'll remember the kind of atmosphere we created, whether it breathed life into others or slowly drained it. We'll reflect on whether our work lifted people up, helped them grow, or left them feeling unseen and worn down.

At the end of it all, what will matter most is not what we built, but *who we built* up along the way.

If we don't address the pain, dysfunction, and disconnection in our workplaces, we risk missing the greater purpose of our influence. We risk leaving behind systems that fracture instead of fortify. We risk watching the next generation, our sons, daughters, coworkers, and mentees, inherit environments that continue to wound what they were born to heal.

I realized that if I truly wanted something better for my children and for the many women and men I've been honored to coach, I couldn't just pray about it. I had to help build it.

This book is my offering, my prayer turned into action. *The Restored Workplace* is a guide for every leader, team member, entrepreneur, and dreamer who senses, deep in their spirit, that something has to change. It's for those who know that the way things are is not the way they have to be.

You are not powerless. You are not stuck. And you are never too small to make a lasting difference. You were placed in your workplace, your business, your school, your community, your ministry, and your circle of influence on purpose. Not to blend in, but to help rebuild.

You were born to be *a Restorer.* The work ahead is sacred. The impact ahead is unstoppable.

And the destiny ahead is divine. It all begins with one healed heart, one courageous decision, and one willing leader, like you. Let's rebuild together, and let's change the world.

INVITATION TO TRANSFORMATION

Invitation to Transformation: Healing People Through Healing Workplaces

The workplace is not just where we earn a paycheck. It is where we spend much of our lives dreaming bold dreams, building meaningful relationships, facing challenges, growing into the leaders and difference-makers we are called to be. It is supposed to be a place where purpose is refined, talents are multiplied, and lives are strengthened.

Yet for far too many people, the workplace has become something very different. Instead of being a place of growth, creativity, and calling, it has become a place of deep stress, silent trauma, and spiritual depletion. A place where people slowly lose their joy, their peace, and too often, even their sense of worth. But it doesn't have to stay this way, and it won't, not if we are willing to contribute to building something better.

Healthy workplaces prioritize the well-being of the people inside them. They refuse to treat employees as machines designed for output. Instead, they see them as what they truly are: living souls with stories, struggles, families, dreams, and destinies. They recognize that every desk, every office, and every conference call is filled not with titles but with human beings created and deeply loved by God.

A truly restored workplace doesn't merely allow healing. It actively supports, cultivates, and celebrates it.

What Healing Workplaces Look Like

Healing workplaces create safe spaces for open communication, where people can speak honestly without fear of retaliation, judgment, or rejection. They foster cultures where difficult conversations are handled with courage, compassion, and dignity, not weaponized against the vulnerable or silenced by fear. Dialogue is not dangerous in these places. It is encouraged, honored, and stewarded with wisdom.

Healing workplaces offer robust mental health resources because they understand that mental wellness is not a luxury but essential to thriving. They provide access to counseling services, employee assistance programs, wellness workshops, and emotional support systems that tear down the stigma surrounding mental health struggles.

In these workplaces, seeking help is seen not as weakness, but as wisdom. Healing workplaces encourage self-care and recovery practices, recognizing that *rest is not laziness but stewardship*. They support rhythms of renewal, honor time off, celebrate healthy boundaries, and refuse to glorify burnout as a badge of honor.

Schedules, policies, and expectations are based on the belief that healthy people create healthy workplaces and that thriving lives outside of work fuel excellence inside of it. In a healing workplace, people are not punished for having needs. They are *equipped and empowered* to meet them.

Biblical Foundations for Healing Workplaces

God has always cared deeply about the restoration and well-being of His people, in every area of life, including where we work. The Bible gives us clear and practical wisdom for how we are called to relate to one another: to carry each other's burdens (Galatians 6:2), to speak words that build up instead of tear down (1 Thessalonians 5:11), and to be peacemakers in every environment we step into (James 3:18).

Jesus modeled this beautifully. He created space for the weary and wounded to find rest, dignity, and renewal, not judgment. He invited people to come just as they were, offering healing where others had only offered pressure or rejection (Matthew 11:28–30).

That same spirit can live in our workplaces today. When we lead with compassion, listen before we react, and choose to build others up instead of tearing them down, we reflect God's heart in real, tangible ways.

This isn't just about better meetings or boosting morale. It's about creating spaces where people feel seen, valued, and whole. Where transformation begins from the inside out. And when we do that, we're not just improving workplace culture, we're joining in something much bigger. We're participating in God's work of restoration on the earth.

As Jesus prayed, "Your kingdom come, Your will be done, on earth as it is in heaven" (Matthew 6:10, AMP). Prioritizing healed workplaces isn't just a good leadership practice. Healed workplaces become sacred spaces, where minds are renewed, hearts are healed, and God's presence can dwell. Where God's presence dwells, peace, purpose, *and yes, even prosperity,* will follow.

Practical Strategies for Healing Workplaces

Restoration doesn't happen by accident. It requires intentional leadership, courageous conversations, and a faith-driven commitment to stewarding people well. Here are several ways to begin cultivating a healing workplace:

1. **Create Brave Spaces for Dialogue**: Hold regular team check-ins where people are invited to share ideas, concerns, and personal experiences without fear of retaliation.

2. **Provide Mental Health Resources**: Partner with counseling services, offer mental wellness days, and, when possible, offer faith-based support that addresses emotional and spiritual healing.

3. **Encourage Healthy Boundaries**: Help leaders and team members understand that rest isn't a sign of weakness; it's a sign of wisdom. Create a culture where caring for your mental, emotional, and spiritual health is not just allowed, but expected.

4. **Honor Sabbath rhythms:** Have intentional times of rest, reflection, and reconnection with God and what matters most. These aren't just about a day off, but about regularly stepping away from constant striving to be renewed from the inside out.

5. **Normalize Saying "No" When Needed:** Give your team permission to protect their energy and priorities. Saying "no" isn't selfish; it's strategic. When people feel the freedom to set healthy boundaries, they're more present, more purposeful, and more passionate about what they do say yes to. Empowering leaders and team members to be selective doesn't hinder progress; it creates room for better decisions, stronger collaboration, and a deeper commitment to the ideas that truly move the mission forward. In the long run, this kind of clarity and intentionality often leads to greater productivity, healthier teams, and even increased profitability.

6. **Model Forgiveness and Grace:** When mistakes happen (and they will), address them with compassion. Encourage reconciliation over retaliation and

humility over pride.

7. **Recognize the Whole Person:** Celebrate not only professional achievements but also family milestones, personal victories, and acts of service that reveal the heart behind the work.

A healing workplace is built on the belief that people are not valuable because of what they produce. They are valuable because of who they are: beloved sons and daughters of God, created for good works (Ephesians 2:10).

An Invitation to You

Healing the workplace is not merely a strategy. It is an act of love, a reflection of heaven. You are invited, not just to hope for a better workplace, but to help create it. You are invited to model a different way of working and leading, rooted in honor, empathy, compassion, truth, and grace.

You are invited to build brave spaces, steward trust, prioritize healing, and champion rest, creativity, and human dignity.

It will not always be easy. Restoration rarely is. But it will be worth it for the lives that are touched, for the dreams that are revived, for the destinies that are unlocked, and for the ripple effect that will reach farther than we can imagine.

Because when workplaces heal, people heal. When people heal, families flourish. When families flourish, communities are rebuilt and transformed. When communities are transformed, the Kingdom of God advances, and the world is positively modified into something powerfully beautiful.

The invitation is here. The time is now. Let's heal workplaces, and in doing so, heal hearts, homes, businesses, and generations to come.

PART I:
THE CRISIS OF BROKEN WORKPLACES

CHAPTER 1

The Silent Epidemic:
Broken Relationships in the Modern Workplace

You don't have to work in a toxic office to know the sting of broken workplace relationships. Sometimes, the wounds are obvious: the gossiping coworker, the passive-aggressive emails, the boss who leads through fear rather than inspiration.

But often, the brokenness is far more subtle. The quiet misunderstandings that are never addressed, the resentment that slowly simmers beneath the surface, and the trust that was never fully built, or worse, is quickly broken. The unspoken tension that drains the joy out of collaboration and the silent competition that turns teammates into reluctant rivals.

Broken relationships are the silent epidemic infecting workplaces around the world. They drain energy, crush creativity, delay destinies, and diminish the very purpose for which God calls people into work in the first place.

If we don't address the brokenness, we don't just risk losing profits or productivity. We risk losing people, and their dreams, their gifts, their talents, their abilities, and their hearts.

Where the Breakdown Begins

The breakdown of workplace relationships rarely happens overnight. It is often a slow erosion caused by familiar culprits, the patterns we see over and over again across industries and offices:

1. **Poor Communication**: When communication is unclear, inconsistent, or absent, confusion grows, assumptions multiply, and trust erodes. Proverbs 15:1 reminds us, "A gentle answer turns away wrath, but a harsh word stirs up anger." In the absence of thoughtful, courageous communication, conflict isn't resolved; it is fueled.

2. **Lack of Trust**: Trust is the foundation of every healthy relationship, professional and personal. Without it, collaboration becomes cautious, feedback becomes feared, and teams crumble into isolated silos of survival. Proverbs 11:13 teaches us, "A gossip betrays a confidence, but a trustworthy person keeps a secret." Trust must be intentionally built, consistently protected, and tenderly restored when broken.

3. **Power Imbalances**: When leadership becomes more about domination than *stewardship*, workplaces suffer deeply. Jesus modeled leadership that lifts, not crushes. "The greatest among you must be your servant," He said in Matthew 23:11. Healthy leadership uses authority to elevate others, not to intimidate or control.

4. **Overemphasis on Individual Achievement**: Today's culture often glorifies personal accolades over team success. While individual excellence matters, Philippians 2:4 calls us to "look not only to your own interests, but also to the interests of others." When collaboration is sacrificed on the altar of competition, relationships deteriorate, trust fades, and teams fracture.

5. **Workplace Romances**: Even relationships born

from genuine connection can create unintended tension in professional spaces. Workplace romances often result in favoritism, jealousy, blurred boundaries, and sometimes broken marraiges and relationships as a result. All of the above undermine team trust and cohesion if they are not remedied and navigated with extraordinary wisdom and accountability.

6. **Miscommunication and Assumptions**: A single misunderstood email. A poorly phrased comment. A tone misread through a screen. Without intentionality, minor miscommunications grow into major fractures, causing more pain than anyone ever intended.

Healing the Silent Epidemic

The good news is that **broken workplaces are not beyond redemption.** With intentional strategies rooted in biblical wisdom and empowerment principles, restoration is absolutely possible. Here's how the healing begins:

- **Prioritize Clear, Honest, Loving Communication:** Cultivate a culture of transparency. Train leaders and employees to listen first, to seek clarification before assuming the worst, and to speak the truth in love. James 1:19 reminds us to be "quick to listen, slow to speak, and slow to become angry." Listening is ministry, and clarity is kindness.
- **Rebuild Trust Through Consistency and Integrity:** Trust isn't built overnight. It is built and rebuilt with one consistent word, one matching action, and one protected confidence at a time. Model honesty, celebrate integrity, and promote account-

ability *from the **top** down.*

- **Balance Leadership with Humility:** Leadership must be rooted in service, not superiority. True leaders humbly steward their influence, lifting others higher rather than lording power over them. When leaders see themselves as servants first, entire cultures change.
- **Promote Collaboration Over Competition:** Create goals that require teamwork to achieve. Celebrate team victories publicly and often. Make collaboration a core value woven into promotions, recognition, and rewards.
- **Establish Clear Professional Boundaries:** Healthy workplaces respect emotional and relational boundaries. Clear, fair policies around professionalism protect trust, honor relationships, and foster emotional safety.
- **Normalize Feedback and Conflict Resolution:** Conflict is not the enemy. Unaddressed conflict is. Teach leaders and employees how to approach disagreement biblically: privately, respectfully, promptly. (Matthew 18:15-17 gives a clear blueprint.) Normalize the practice of gentle, honest feedback that corrects without condemning.

What a Healed Workplace Looks Like

When relationships are healed, workplaces are transformed from battlegrounds to gardens. Collaboration becomes effortless, innovation flourishes, and loyalty deepens. People show up with their full, God-given potential, not because they have to, but because they want to. Joy, trust, and excellence cease to be exceptions; they become the culture.

Most importantly, workplaces become places where

destinies are protected, not poisoned, and where people are built up and not broken down. They are places where restoration flows outward, touching individuals, families, and communities beyond what we can see.

Reflection Questions

Take a moment to reflect prayerfully:

1. Where have I experienced broken relationships at work (either as the one wounded or the one who unintentionally wounded others)?
2. In what ways have poor communication, lack of trust, or unhealthy competition affected my workplace experiences?
3. How might God be calling me to be a Restorer in my current workplace, starting today?

Workplace Healing Action Steps

This week, take small but mighty steps toward healing:

- Choose one coworker or team member to encourage genuinely.
- Schedule a 10-minute check-in with someone you've felt distant from.
- Practice active listening in your next meeting; listen without rehearsing your response.
- Speak one life-giving, affirming word over your team or leader.
- Pray daily for your workplace, specifically speaking and asking God to heal hidden wounds and to raise up Restorers.

Destiny Declarations

Speak these aloud and declare them in faith:

- *I am called to be a Restorer in my home, workplace, and every place I serve.*
- *I build bridges, not barriers, with my words and actions.*
- *Through God's wisdom and love, I help heal broken places.*

Workplace Restoration Toolkit (Appendix Reference)

In the Appendix, you'll find practical tools to help you begin:

- *A Sample Dialogue for Healing Miscommunication*
- *A Trust-Building Activity for Teams*
- *A Guide for Conflict Resolution Conversations*
- *Prayer Prompts for Workplace Restoration*

(See Appendix A: Workplace Restoration Toolkit to start rebuilding today.)

Prayer for Healing Broken Relationships in the Workplace

Heavenly Father,

You are the God of restoration, the One who binds up the brokenhearted and breathes life into dry places. Today, I bring before You the hidden fractures, unspoken tensions, and silent wounds that exist within my workplace. I may not have all the words, all the answers, or even all the strength, but I know You do.

Lord, I ask You to search my heart. Show me where I've held on to offense, where I've avoided the hard conversations, where I've spoken out of fear instead of faith. Forgive me for the moments I've contributed to the brokenness through silence, gossiping, judgment, or self-protection. Heal what I can't fix. Mend what I've missed.

I surrender the people I work with, every coworker, every leader, every team member, into Your hands. You see what I cannot. You understand what I don't. Help me to see them as You do: not as rivals or obstacles, but as image-bearers worthy of honor, healing, and hope.

Father, give me the grace to speak truth in love. The humility to listen without defense. The courage to rebuild trust brick by brick. Help me to be willing to work at it. Grant me the patience to navigate complexity with compassion. And the boldness to be *a Restorer*, even when it's uncomfortable or unreciprocated.

Let my words carry healing, my presence disarm fear, and my work be a vessel of peace in a place that has known tension for too long.

I declare that my workplace is not too far gone, that healing is possible, and that I am being sent not just to do a job but to carry Your heart into every hallway, every meeting, and every relationship.

Use me, Lord, as a Restorer, not in my strength, but in Yours. And let the transformation begin with me.

In Jesus' Name, Amen.

CHAPTER 2

Beyond Profit:
The Human Cost of a Broken Work Culture

If you want to truly understand the health of a workplace, don't just examine its profit margins. Look at its people.

While numbers may reveal the bottom line, people reveal an organization's soul, and it's source of life (or its reason for death).

Behind polished reports, branding strategies, and smiling press releases, many workplaces today are hiding a silent epidemic: an epidemic of anxiety, frustration, anger, and emotional exhaustion. And the ripple effects are devastating.

When the culture of a workplace is broken, it doesn't just hinder the company's financial success. It steals joy, delays dreams, and fractures relationships. And it robs people of the energy they need to fulfill their God-given purpose.

Again, this is not just about spreadsheets and balance sheets. It is about souls, living, breathing, dreaming people who are silently suffering under cultures that value profits over people and performance over purpose.

The Emotional Fallout: How Broken Cultures Break People

Workplace anxiety extends far beyond tight deadlines or packed schedules. It often stems from environments where fear replaces trust, where poor communication breeds confusion, and where isolation takes the place of healthy collaboration.

Over time, this kind of atmosphere wears people down. It causes both employees and leaders to operate in survival mode: masking their stress, suppressing their emotions, and sometimes turning to unhealthy or even addictive coping mechanisms just to get through the day.

For some, waking up each morning feels like gearing up for battle, mentally, emotionally, and spiritually. The workplace becomes something to endure, not a space to grow.

When anxiety becomes the norm, creativity is stifled, relationships suffer, and people begin to shrink back from their full potential. That's why *addressing the emotional climate of a workplace isn't optional; **it's essential.***

When people experience persistent stress at work, they shift into emotional survival mode, constantly guarding themselves, anticipating conflict, questioning their worth, and doubting their safety.

Frustration builds when expectations are unclear, leadership feels absent or unfair, and employees feel trapped between unrealistic demands and limited support. Anger festers when people feel ignored, mistreated, or betrayed by those entrusted to lead and protect them. Eventually, the emotional turmoil spills outward, infecting teams, departments, and entire organizations.

Workplaces become battlegrounds. Innovation dies. Trust disintegrates. People who once entered their roles full of passion and promise now carry silent wounds that no one sees, but everyone feels.

The Real Cost of Poor Morale

Poor morale isn't just a "soft issue." It's a serious, deeply rooted problem with very real consequences that affects every level of an organization.

When morale is low, people don't just feel it; they live it:

- Employees begin to dread coming to work, leading to higher absenteeism, or worse, presenteeism where they're physically present but mentally checked out.
- Creativity withers because innovation can't thrive in an atmosphere of fear, pressure, or constant criticism.
- Collaboration breaks down as teammates start seeing each other as threats instead of partners.
- Leadership credibility erodes because people don't follow titles; they follow trust.
- Productivity slows. Energy drains, and even the most loyal hearts start to grow tired.

Scripture speaks directly to this in Proverbs 17:22: "A joyful heart is good medicine, but a crushed spirit dries up the bones." When a workplace is filled with crushed spirits, joy evaporates and dries up, and with it, engagement, trust, and commitment.

Eventually, the company doesn't just lose momentum; it begins to lose its soul. Not because of a broken business model, but because of broken people within it. Low morale isn't just a threat to performance. *It's a warning sign* that hearts need healing, and the culture needs to be restored.

The Hidden Toll of High Turnover

Eventually, people who are not appreciated reach a breaking point. And they leave. Good hearts and exceptional talent leave. And when they leave, they take far more than just their labor with them.

High turnover drains organizations of their:

- **Institutional Knowledge:** the wisdom, insights, and relationships built over the years are lost.
- **Team Stability:** Every departure destabilizes trust and rhythm within the team.
- **Financial Resources:** Recruiting, onboarding, and retraining new employees is costly, often thousands of dollars per hire.
- **Emotional Resilience:** those who stay are left carrying heavier burdens, questioning whether they should leave, too.

Galatians 6:9 encourages us, "Let us not grow weary of doing good, for in due season we will reap, if we do not give up."

But far too often, good employees do give up. Not because they lack grit or calling, but because they lack a healthy environment where their soul is nourished as much as their skill is valued.

If we allow our workplaces to become environments of constant loss, emotional depletion, and unhealed wounds, even the strongest hearts eventually grow weary.

Healing the Human Cost

True restoration begins with a shift in perspective: Our greatest asset isn't our products, services, or bottom line; it's our people.

Companies don't grow on their own; their people grow first. Organizations don't succeed in a vacuum; people succeed first. Cultures don't heal automatically; people heal first.

If we want to see lasting change in the workplace, we

need to return to what God has always shown us through His Word:

- Leadership rooted in humility.
- Stewardship grounded in compassion.
- Honor that's freely given.
- And love that's visible, not just in words, but in how we show up and serve each other daily.

Healing begins when we stop seeing people as job titles or metrics and start seeing them as whole, God-created beings: sons and daughters, parents and caretakers, dreamers, creatives, and future leaders.

It begins when we take time to truly listen, not just to respond, but to understand. "Be quick to listen, slow to speak, and slow to become angry." (James 1:19).

It begins when we lead with integrity, fairness, and consistency, mirroring the faithfulness of God in our leadership. "Because of the Lord's great love we are not consumed, for his compassions never fail. They are new every morning." (Lamentations 3:22–23).

Healing begins when we choose collaboration over competition, recognizing that every role on the team is vital to the shared mission. As Romans 12:4–5 reminds us, 'Just as each of us has one body with many members... so in Christ we, though many, form one body.'

It also begins when we elevate emotional, mental, and spiritual well-being, not as luxuries or optional perks, but as non-negotiable priorities. Because when people thrive, organizations flourish, whether in business, community, ministry, or any mission field.

Restored workplaces intentionally create rhythms of restoration. They foster cultures where people are seen, heard, valued, and empowered, rather than being used, overlooked, or burned out.

They reject the world's obsession with hustle and burn-out, and instead embrace God's design for wholeness and flourishing. Because when people truly thrive, workplaces don't just survive. They flourish in ways no spreadsheet can measure, but eternity will never forget.

Reflection Questions

Take a few moments to reflect:

1. Have I ever worked in an environment where poor morale drained my energy or joy?
2. What did I learn from that experience?
3. How have I seen high turnover impact a team's stability, trust, and spirit?
4. In my current role, what small ways can I start raising morale and healing broken dynamics?

Workplace Healing Action Steps

This week, take intentional steps toward creating a healing atmosphere:

- Genuinely encourage one colleague who seems overwhelmed, unnoticed, or discouraged.
- Suggest or organize a small team appreciation gesture: a lunch, a handwritten thank-you card, a simple recognition of someone's effort.
- If you are in leadership, consider conducting a short, anonymous pulse survey asking employees: "What would make you feel more supported and valued here?"
- Sometimes the smallest seeds of encouragement grow into the mightiest trees of restoration.

Destiny Declarations

Speak these aloud and sow them into your workplace atmosphere:

- *I am a carrier of encouragement and hope in my workplace.*
- *I build environments where people feel seen, valued, and empowered.*
- *Through Christ, I have the wisdom, strength, and compassion to help heal what's broken around me.*

Workplace Restoration Toolkit (Appendix Reference)

For additional tools and resources, visit the Appendix, where you'll find:

- *Sample Employee Engagement Survey*
- *Quick Guide: How to Encourage a Discouraged Team Member*
- *Checklist for Building a Culture of Honor*

(See Appendix A: Workplace Restoration Toolkit to begin creating a healthier culture today.)

Prayer for Healing Broken Work Cultures and Restoring People Over Profit

Gracious God,

You are the God who sees. You see beyond performance metrics, titles, and bottom lines. You see hearts. You see the unspoken weariness in the eyes of Your people, the hidden battles behind polite smiles, and the quiet resignation in those who once walked into work full of dreams and purpose.

Lord, we bring before You the heavy cost of broken workplace culture, the stress that steals our joy, the silence that suffocates creativity, the competition that divides teams, and the burnout that leaves even the strongest souls exhausted. We grieve the invisible toll that anxiety, confusion, and poor morale have taken on hearts across every industry.

Yet, we do not grieve without hope because You, God, are a Restorer. You bring beauty from ashes and healing from despair. You care not just about what we build but also how we build it, and whether our workplaces reflect the Kingdom principles of compassion, unity, and honor.

So today, Father, I ask that You start the restoration work in me. Make me more sensitive to the pain around me. Help me see the discouraged teammate, the overwhelmed leader, and the overlooked intern, not as roles or job titles but as souls carrying burdens I may never fully understand.

Where morale is low, help me be a voice of encouragement. Where tension is thick, help me bring peace and clarity. Where turnover and loss have shaken trust, help me plant seeds of stability and honor.

Lord, teach me to lead with a servant's heart, whether I hold a formal title or not. Give me the courage to advocate for people, not just performance… for healing, not just hustle… for value that flows from identity, not productivity.

Let my words be healing, and my actions honoring. Let my workplace be transformed not because I waited for someone else to fix it, but because I said "yes" to You and carried Your heart into every hallway and team I touched.

Help me live the truth that cultures don't shift on accident; they shift when people carry light into dark places.

And today, I declare: I am one of those people. I am a light carrier and a Restorer. And this is my assignment.

In Jesus' Name, Amen.

CHAPTER 3

Trust, Safety, Purpose:
The Real Bottom Line

It's often said that trust moves at the speed of relationships, not results, and it's true. Trust isn't built by performance alone; it grows through meaningful connection. It develops when people invest time in honest communication, empathy, and shared experiences.

You can meet deadlines, hit targets, and achieve impressive outcomes, but if people feel unseen, unheard, or simply used, trust will still be lacking.

In the healthiest workplaces, trust isn't a buzzword or an afterthought. It's the invisible foundation that supports everything else, culture, collaboration, and long-term success.

Without trust, even the most talented teams falter, even the most brilliant strategies collapse, and even the most profitable organizations eventually lose what matters most: *their people.*

Trust is not optional. It is essential. It is built or broken in every conversation, policy, decision, and leadership moment.

How Lack of Trust Destroys Workplaces

When an organization lacks trust, it creates a silent but deadly culture of fear and self-protection. Employees begin to play it safe, feeling it's smarter to cover up mistakes than admit them. They withhold feedback, ideas, and themselves; not because they don't care, but because they don't feel safe. The flow of innovation, creativity, and courage slows to a trickle.

The top reasons for trust erosion include poor communication, micromanagement, inconsistent leadership, unchecked toxic behavior, lack of transparency, and a failure to listen or follow through on promises. Unchecked, these patterns create a breeding ground for disengagement, division, and organizational disaster.

Proverbs 11:14, AMP reminds us, "Where there is no [wise, intelligent] guidance, the people fall [and go off course like a ship without a helm], But in the abundance of [wise and godly] counselors there is victory."

Without trust, there is no proper guidance, only suspicion, fear, and a slow, silent stagnation.

The Cost of Allowing Toxic Behavior

When toxic behavior is allowed to take root, it sends a chilling message to every team member: "You are not safe here." And trust, once lost, is never easily regained. When bullies, manipulators, or gossipers are left unchecked:

- High performers, the very people organizations most need, are often the first to leave.
- Remaining employees stop offering ideas or speaking up, knowing it's safer to stay silent.
- Trust evaporates, not just toward the toxic individual but also toward leadership.
- Quiet resentment grows into active disengagement, as people mentally check out even before their resignation letters are written.

Ephesians 4:29, AMP commands us, "Do not let unwholesome [foul, profane, worthless, vulgar] words ever come out of your mouth, but only such speech as is good for building up others, according to the need and the occasion, so that it will be a blessing to those who hear [you speak]."

Healthy workplaces confront toxicity boldly but compassionately, building environments where people are protected, honored, and built up instead of broken down.

The Trap of Micromanagement

Micromanagement is not about excellence; it's about fear. Leaders who micromanage often believe they are helping, but in truth, they undermine employee confidence, destroy a sense of ownership, diminish creativity, and suffocate initiative.

When leaders assign roles but then immediately take over, they send a devastating message:

- "I don't trust you."
- "You're not good enough."
- "Your ideas aren't welcome here."

Over time, employees begin to second-guess themselves, withdraw emotionally, and lose trust in their leaders and their own abilities.

Healthy leadership, however, trusts others to grow, even through mistakes. Paul exhorted young Timothy, "Let no one despise your youth, but set the believers an example in speech, in conduct, in love, in faith, in purity." (1 Timothy 4:12). Trust must be extended as a gift long before it ever blossoms into fruit.

Safety First: The Foundation of Growth

If trust is the foundation, then psychological safety is the air we breathe. Psychological safety, the belief that you can speak up, take risks, and admit mistakes without fear of humiliation or retaliation, is the strongest predictor of high-performing, innovative, and resilient teams.

Key elements that shape a thriving culture of safety include:

1. **Management Commitment and Employee Involvement:** Leaders must model humility, consistency, and courage, creating environments that celebrate honesty and growth.
2. **Worksite Safety Analysis:** Organizations must consistently examine not just physical hazards but relational hazards, such as favoritism, broken systems, and hidden resentments.
3. **Hazard Prevention and Control:** To protect the team, toxic behaviors and unhealthy patterns must be addressed quickly and firmly.
4. **Safety and Health Training:** To thrive, employees must be equipped with skills and emotional, relational, and mental health support.

Healthy workplaces are not built passively. They are cultivated intentionally, courageously, and prayerfully, one conversation, policy, and decision at a time.

Solutions for Building Trust, Safety, and Purpose

Building restored workplaces doesn't happen overnight. But it begins with simple, courageous, Spirit-led actions that can start today.

- **Encourage Feedback:** Create safe, structured spaces for employees to share ideas, concerns, and feedback without fear of retaliation. "Listen to advice and accept instruction, that you may gain wisdom in the future." (Proverbs 19:20).

- **Communicate Effectively:** Clear is kind. Set clear goals, expectations, and roles. Listen deeply. Speak truth gently.
- **Follow Through on Commitments:** Say what you mean, and mean what you say. Credibility is built through consistency more than charisma.
- **Open Communication:** Model honest, respectful dialogue at all levels. Normalize truth-telling with kindness.
- **Build Trust Gradually:** Be patient. Trust grows through a thousand small moments of reliability and grace.
- **Psychological Safety:** Reward vulnerability. Create a culture where asking questions, sharing mistakes, and offering ideas are celebrated, not punished.
- **Admit Your Mistakes:** Leaders must model humility. "Confess your sins to one another and pray for one another, that you may be healed." (James 5:16)
- **Be Honest:** Speak the truth consistently, clearly, lovingly.
- **Be Vulnerable:** Let people see your humanity. Vulnerability invites authenticity.
- **Demonstrate Empathy:** Before fixing, seek to understand. "Rejoice with those who rejoice; mourn with those who mourn." (Romans 12:15).
- **Lead by Example:** Integrity is not telling people what to do, it's *showing* them how to live.
- **Model Trustworthy Behavior:** Keep confidences, keep promises, and own your shortcomings.
- **Practice Inclusive Decision-Making:** Value the

wisdom, perspectives, and experiences around you.

- **Set Clear Expectations:** Ambiguity breeds anxiety. Clarity breeds confidence.
- **Share Important Information:** Empower others by being open, not secretive.
- **Transparency:** Help others understand the "why" behind your decisions. Transparency builds trust faster than explanations ever will.
- **Acknowledge Emotions:** Honor how people feel, without judgment or minimization.
- **Answer Team Building Questions:** Use team-building conversations to uncover dreams, fears, strengths, and growth areas.
- **Collaboration:** Celebrate partnerships and group wins as loudly as individual achievements.
- **Encourage Employees' Share of Voice:** Actively solicit and honor diverse opinions, even when they challenge your own.
- **Engage Employees on Their Terms:** Learn how people prefer to connect and build trust in personalized ways.
- **Extend Trust to Others:** Offer trust as a gift, not a reward. Trust begets trust.
- **Foster a Sense of Belonging:** Create a community where everyone knows, "You are seen. You are needed. You are valued."
- **Get to Know Each Other:** Invest relationally. Relationship always precedes collaboration.

Reflection Questions

Take a few minutes to reflect prayerfully:

1. Where in my workplace do I see trust lacking?

2. What small action could I take today to build trust and safety with one person?
3. How can I model vulnerability, humility, and empathy in my leadership or service?

Workplace Healing Action Steps

This week, make a deliberate choice to cultivate trust and safety:

- In your next meeting, practice listening without interrupting or correcting.
- Share one area where you need help or feedback to model vulnerability.
- Invite one coworker's honest opinion on a project or decision, and thank them genuinely for their insight.

Destiny Declarations

Speak these aloud over your workplace and your calling:

- *I am a builder of trust and a cultivator of purpose.*
- *I create safe spaces where God's gifts and destinies can thrive.*
- *Through Christ, I lead with humility, courage, and love.*

Workplace Restoration Toolkit (Appendix Reference)

Visit the Appendix for practical tools to help you:

- *Trust-Building Exercises for Teams*
- *Sample Feedback Invitation Templates*
- *Psychological Safety Assessment Worksheet*

(See Appendix A: Workplace Restoration Toolkit to start today.)

Prayer of Trust, Safety & Purpose in the Workplace

Heavenly Father,

You are the Master Architect of restoration. You design every life and every workplace with purpose, order, and love. Today, I come before You as Your servant, willing, humbled, and ready to be used as a vessel of healing in the place where I work.

Lord, I lift up my workplace to You, every hallway, every conference room, every computer screen, and every desk. You see what I cannot. You hear every unspoken fear and every whispered frustration. You know where trust has been broken, safety has been compromised, and purpose has been buried beneath stress, silence, and fear.

Father, start with me. Teach me how to build trust not just with my words but also with my consistency, humility, and heart. Where fear has caused me to shrink back, please give me courage. Where past wounds have made me guarded, provide me with grace to open up again, with wisdom but without walls.

Help me to listen deeply, speak truth kindly, apologize quickly, forgive fully, and lead by example, not by ego. May I become a living picture of the kind of culture I long to see, honest, healing, and safe.

Lord, break the strongholds of micromanagement, secrecy, and competition that strangle creativity and kill collaboration. In their place, plant *trust, transparency, and teamwork.* Raise up leaders who humbly steward power, protect people with honor, and promote purpose over performance.

I ask for *psychological safety* to flood my workplace like a river so that my coworkers would feel seen, heard, and free to bring their whole selves to the table. May vulnerability no longer be feared, but celebrated. May mistakes become moments for growth, not shame.

Jesus, You are the Shepherd who restores souls. Restore our workplace, restore our relationships, and restore our purpose.

Let my presence at work become an invitation, a doorway to peace, clarity, and healing. Please make me a Restorer. Let trust rise again where it has fallen. Let safety take root where fear once ruled. And let purpose awaken in every heart that has grown weary.

Use me, Lord, as an agent of Kingdom culture, not just to do a job, but to create an atmosphere where destinies are fulfilled and people are healed.

I surrender this assignment to You.

In Jesus' Name, Amen.

PART II:
FOUNDATIONS OF RESTORATION

CHAPTER 4

Emotional Intelligence:
The Core Skill of the Restored Workplace

The Role of Emotional Intelligence in a Restored Workplace

If trust is the foundation of every restored workplace, then *emotional intelligence* is the skill that keeps that foundation solid and lasting.

Without it, trust is fragile, easily broken by miscommunication, stress, or pride. But with emotional intelligence, trust becomes resilient. Relationships deepen. Teams don't just survive challenges, they thrive through them.

Emotional intelligence (often referred to as EI) is the ability to understand, manage, and respond wisely to one's own emotions and those of others. It's not about being overly emotional. It's about being spiritually and relationally wise, able to discern the emotional undercurrents that influence every conversation, decision, and interaction.

Scripture tells us:

If any of you lacks wisdom {to guide him through a decision or circumstance}, he is to ask of {our benevolent} God, who gives to everyone generously and without rebuke or blame, and it will be given to him. —James 1:5, AMP

In emotionally intelligent workplaces where wisdom is sought out, communication flows more freely. Conflicts are approached with grace instead of defensiveness. Collaboration becomes natural. And trust grows, like a well-watered garden.

But where emotional intelligence is lacking, even the most talented teams struggle. Misunderstandings multiply. Egos collide. Tension goes unresolved. The culture starts to break down from the inside out.

If we truly want to restore our workplaces, we must begin by restoring emotional health. And that starts with emotional intelligence, wisdom in action, guided by the Spirit, shaping how we lead, listen, and love in the places we've been called to serve.

Why Emotional Intelligence Matters

When relationships break down in the workplace, it's rarely because of a lack of skill. It's almost always because of a lack of understanding, empathy, or wise communication. Scripture teaches us, "A fool vents all his feelings, but a wise man holds them back." (Proverbs 29:11, NKJV).

Emotional intelligence teaches us to steward our emotions, rather than being ruled by them. It empowers us to build others up instead of tearing them down in moments of frustration or fear.

Individuals with strong emotional intelligence can:

- Understand and regulate their own emotions with maturity and grace.
- Recognize and empathize with the feelings of others, even when experiences differ.
- Communicate with clarity, compassion, and courage.
- Handle conflict without escalating it into division.

- Inspire trust and foster collaboration.
- Create positive, empowering environments where people feel safe to bring their whole selves to work.

Emotional intelligence ultimately leads to better teamwork, increased productivity, higher job satisfaction, more decisive leadership, and workplaces where people and purpose thrive.

Key Components of Emotional Intelligence in the Workplace

Developing emotional intelligence isn't reserved for managers or HR professionals. It's a critical skill for every person who longs to build relationships that heal rather than harm.

The four key components are:

1. *Self-Awareness:* Recognizing your own emotions, triggers, strengths, and growth areas, without shame, defensiveness, or denial.
2. *Self-Management:* Regulating your emotional responses, choosing self-control over reaction, staying calm under pressure, and responding with wisdom.
3. *Social Awareness:* Accurately perceiving and empathizing with the emotions and experiences of others, even when they don't mirror your own.
4. *Relationship Management:* Navigating conflicts wisely, communicating clearly, inspiring trust, encouraging growth, and strengthening connections over time.

Proverbs 15:1 offers timeless wisdom for every workplace: "A gentle answer turns away wrath, but a harsh word stirs up anger."

Those with high emotional intelligence know how to bring peace into heated moments, clarity into confusion, and hope into even the most difficult conversations.

Applying Emotional Intelligence to Restore Workplaces

Restoring broken workplace relationships requires more than technical skills or new policies.

It requires emotional healing through wisdom, humility, and courageous love. Emotional intelligence helps rebuild trust and mutual respect by empowering people to engage in:

1. **Open Communication:** Creating environments where people feel genuinely heard, valued, and respected. Emotionally intelligent leaders listen actively, ask clarifying questions, and ensure every voice has a seat at the table.

2. **Active Listening:** True listening isn't waiting for your turn to speak. It's entering into another person's experience with empathy and openness. James 1:19 exhorts us: "Everyone should be quick to listen, slow to speak, and slow to become angry."

3. **Willingness to Understand Different Perspectives:** Emotionally intelligent individuals don't react defensively when they are challenged. They pause, seek to understand, and lean into learning, even when it's uncomfortable.

4. **Seeking Outside Support When Needed:** Sometimes healing requires the humility to admit, "I can't fix this alone." Whether through coaching,

counseling, mediation, or mentorship, wise leaders know that asking for help is not weakness; it's wisdom.

5. **Finding Common Ground:** Instead of focusing on what divides, emotionally intelligent teams identify what unites. Shared goals, common values, and a vision for mutual success become the glue that holds them together.

Practical Outcomes of Emotional Intelligence in Workplaces

When emotional intelligence is practiced daily and modeled from leadership downward:

- Conflict becomes an opportunity for growth rather than a breeding ground for resentment.
- Communication becomes clearer, more compassionate, and more courageous.
- Collaboration flows naturally, fueled by trust rather than suspicion.
- Productivity rises because emotional energy isn't wasted on drama and defensiveness.
- Morale soars because people feel truly seen, heard, and valued.
- Purpose flourishes when people align not just their tasks but their hearts with the work they do.

In short, emotional intelligence doesn't just restore workplaces. It revives them spiritually, relationally, and organizationally.

Reflection Questions

Take a few moments to reflect prayerfully:

1. How well do I recognize and manage my own emotions at work?
2. How often do I seek to understand others before trying to be understood myself?
3. Where can I apply emotional intelligence today to restore trust or strengthen a relationship in my workplace?

Workplace Healing Action Steps

Choose one or more of these action steps to practice this week. In your next conversation:

1. Practice active listening and reflect on what you heard before responding.
2. Identify one emotional trigger that often causes you frustration at work.
3. Pray about it and create a strategy to react calmly next time.
4. Ask a trusted coworker or mentor for honest feedback about how you handle emotions and communication under pressure.

Remember growth begins with small, consistent, courageous choices.

Destiny Declarations

Speak these aloud over yourself and your workplace:

- *Through Christ, I am wise, compassionate, and courageous.*

- *I use my words to heal, not to harm.*
- *I create environments of trust, safety, and collaboration wherever I go.*

Workplace Restoration Toolkit (Appendix Reference)

In the Appendix, you'll find additional resources to support your emotional intelligence journey:

- *Emotional Intelligence Self-Assessment*
- *Sample Active Listening Exercise for Teams*
- *Emotional Triggers Journal Template*

(See Appendix A: Workplace Restoration Toolkit for tools you can use immediately.)

Prayer for Emotional Intelligence and Workplace Restoration

Heavenly Father,

You are the Author of wisdom, the Giver of understanding, and the One who searches hearts and knows our deepest emotions. Today, I come before You asking for the courage and humility to grow in emotional intelligence; not for self-glory, but so I may reflect Your love in how I lead, listen, and live.

Lord, teach me to pause before I react, listen before speaking, and seek understanding before assuming. Help me recognize my emotions without shame and steward them with maturity. Give me grace to manage frustration with peace, to navigate conflict with wisdom, and to respond to others with empathy and honor.

Please make me a vessel of gentleness and discernment in a world that often rewards harshness and defensiveness.

Let my words heal, not harm. Let my presence bring peace, not pressure. Let my leadership build bridges, not barriers.

God, I pray not only for myself but for my entire workplace. Breathe Your Spirit into every office, every meeting, every conversation. Restore trust where it's been broken. Rebuild safety where it's been violated. Reignite purpose where it's been lost.

Help me create space where others can be fully seen, heard, and valued. Let emotional intelligence not be just a skill I master, but a fruit I bear because I walk with You.

May my workplace reflect Heaven, where love leads, grace flows, and every person is treated with dignity and care.

In Jesus' Name, Amen.

CHAPTER 5

Building and Rebuilding Trust

Trust: The Oxygen of a Healthy Workplace

Trust is the oxygen every healthy workplace needs to thrive. Without it, teams begin to suffocate. Creativity withers. Collaboration breaks down, replaced by competition, self-protection, and quiet resignation.

Trust doesn't appear automatically. It isn't built through job titles, shared Zoom calls, or proximity in an office. And once broken, it doesn't simply return on its own; it must be rebuilt with care, humility, and intention.

In today's fast-paced, constantly shifting work environments with hybrid teams, evolving cultures, and relentless demands, trust must be more than a value. It must become a daily discipline.

Trust must be cultivated through consistent words and actions. It must be protected through honesty, integrity, and accountability. And when it's wounded, it must be courageously repaired with humility, patience, and grace.

Building trust isn't a one-time task to check off a leadership list. It's a way of life. It's the ongoing decision to lead with transparency, show up with integrity, extend grace, and love people well, even in the workplace. Because where trust lives, people breathe easier and everything begins to flourish.

Why Trust Is So Fragile, and So Vital

In today's high-pressure work environments, trust can be broken in an instant, and it's often the small moments that do the most damage.

A leader fails to follow through on a promise. A team member vents behind someone's back instead of addressing the issue with honesty and transparency. An employee hides a mistake, not out of malice, but out of fear.

Each moment may seem minor in isolation, but together, they create silent cracks in the foundation. Over time, those cracks widen. They turn vibrant cultures into cautious ones, where people second-guess, stay silent, and stop bringing their best.

Proverbs 10:9 offers a timeless truth: "Whoever walks in integrity walks securely, but he who makes his ways crooked will be found out."

Integrity is the anchor that holds trust in place. It's not perfection; *it's consistency.* It's showing up with honesty, owning our shortcomings, and choosing truth even when it's uncomfortable.

When integrity is present, people feel safe. When it's missing, fear grows. Division grows. And ultimately, destiny is delayed.

That's why trust can't be an afterthought. It must be a priority. Because trust isn't just vital for productivity; it's essential for purpose.

Building Trust in the Modern Workplace

In today's diverse, dynamic, and sometimes remote work environments, building trust requires intentional and continual effort across four key areas:

1. Consistent Action

Consistency is the secret ingredient to credibility. When leaders and teammates consistently follow through on their word, complete tasks with excellence, and show up with dependable character day after day, trust grows strong and deep. People don't trust perfection. They trust predictability, knowing that your behavior will align with your values.

Empowerment Strategy: It's not grand gestures that build trust; it's small, daily acts of faithfulness: returning emails when you promise, honoring deadlines, protecting confidential information.

Biblical Wisdom: "But let your statement be, 'Yes, yes' or 'No, no' [a firm yes or no]; anything more than that comes from the evil one." — Matthew 5:37, AMP

2. Open Communication

Trust cannot survive without honest, clear, and courageous communication. In environments where feedback is feared, silence festers into resentment. Healthy communication means listening patiently, speaking truth in love (Ephesians 4:15), clarifying expectations before misunderstandings arise, and addressing conflicts quickly with kindness.

Empowerment Strategy: Normalize open dialogue. Make no topic "too small" or "too awkward" to be discussed honestly and respectfully.

3. Commitment to Accountability

Real trust grows when everyone, especially leaders,

commits to being held accountable. Accountability is not punishment; it's love. It says, *"I care about you and our mission enough to expect honesty, humility, and growth."* Leaders must lead the way by owning their mistakes, inviting feedback, making corrections without defensiveness, and offering sincere apologies when needed.

Biblical Wisdom: "Better is open rebuke than hidden love." — Proverbs 27:5, NIV

4. Transparency and Vulnerability

Transparency builds trust by letting people into the *"why"* behind decisions, not just the outcomes. Vulnerability invites connection by showing that leadership isn't about having all the answers, but about walking humbly alongside others.

Empowerment Strategy: When appropriate, let your team hear you say, "I don't have all the answers, but I'm committed to finding them with you."

Biblical Wisdom: "Therefore, confess your sins to one another [your false steps, your offenses], and pray for one another, that you may be healed and restored. The heartfelt and persistent prayer of a righteous man (believer) can accomplish much [when put into action and made effective by God—it is dynamic and can have tremendous power]." James 5:16, AMP.

Rebuilding Trust When It's Broke

No workplace is perfect. No leader is flawless. No team is immune to disappointment. But the beauty of God's restoration is that broken trust can be rebuilt, and sometimes, what grows back is even stronger than what was lost.

Here's how to begin:

1. **Acknowledge the Break:** Ignoring the fracture only deepens the wound. Healing begins with courageous honesty: *"Something was broken here. I see it. I own it."*
2. **Apologize and Ask for Forgiveness:** An authentic apology, free of excuses, invites healing and clears space for restoration.
3. **Repair with Actions, Not Just Words:** Promises heal nothing without follow-through. Demonstrate your change over time. Let your actions speak louder than your words.
4. **Invite Dialogue:** Allow the hurt party to share openly, and listen without defensiveness. Understand that the *impact* often speaks louder than our original intentions.
5. **Be Patient:** Trust is earned in drops and lost in buckets. It takes time to rebuild, but *daily consistency*, humility, and faithfulness will win hearts again.

Micro-Moments That Build or Break Trust

Trust isn't built in grand gestures. It's built, or broken, in the small, often unnoticed moments of everyday work life. These micro-moments may seem insignificant in the moment, but over time, they tell the truth about a workplace culture and the people shaping it.

Moments that Build Trust:

- Following through on what you said you'd do, even when it's inconvenient.
- Admitting a mistake without blame-shifting.
- Giving credit where credit is due.
- Speaking to someone directly instead of talking about them to others.
- Responding with grace rather than defensiveness.
- Creating space for others' ideas, even when they differ from your own.
- Protecting someone's dignity, even in correction.

Moments that Break Trust:

- Promising feedback or support, then going silent.
- Dismissing someone's concerns or interrupting their voice.
- Taking credit for a team effort without acknowledgment.
- Talking about people instead of talking to them.
- Reacting harshly when someone is vulnerable.
- Making decisions in secret that affect others publicly.
- Choosing image over integrity.

These moments often happen in passing, but their impact lingers. They can either create an environment of emotional safety or one of quiet suspicion.

That's why cultivating trust isn't just a leadership task. It's a daily practice of integrity, empathy, and courage. It's learning to see every interaction as an opportunity to build something eternal.

*He who is faithful in a very little thing is also faithful in much;
and he who is dishonest in a very little thing is also dishonest in
much. —Luke 16:10, AMP*

Practical Applications for Leaders and Teams

To build and rebuild trust in tangible ways:

- **Encourage Feedback:** Regularly invite open, honest feedback, and listen with a heart to understand.
- **Communicate Effectively:** Clear communication prevents confusion and resentment before they take root.
- **Follow Through on Commitments:** Broken promises break trust. Faithfulness mends it.
- **Practice Transparency:** Share the "why" behind decisions, not just the "what."
- **Demonstrate Empathy:** Lead with your heart as much as your head.
- **Admit Mistakes Quickly:** Humility accelerates healing.
- **Celebrate Team Wins:** Shared success builds shared trust and pride.

Reflection Questions

Take time to consider prayerfully:

1. Where have I unintentionally contributed to broken trust at work?
2. What consistent action can I begin this week to rebuild credibility and care with my team?
3. How can I create more open, transparent communication opportunities in my workplace or leadership

role?

Workplace Healing Action Steps

This week, *set a trust-building goal:*

- Open your office door for open conversations.
- Celebrate a team member's unseen contribution.
- Choose one coworker you need to reconnect with, and take the first small step.
- In your next meeting, share a decision and the heart and "why" behind it.

Small seeds of trust, planted faithfully, grow mighty forests of restoration.

Destiny Declaration

Speak these aloud over yourself and your workplace:

- *Through Christ, I am a safe place for trust to grow.*
- *I lead and work with integrity, humility, and compassion.*
- *Each day, I help rebuild what was broken and restore what was lost.*

Workplace Restoration Toolkit (Appendix Reference)

In the Appendix, you'll find ready-to-use resources to support your journey:

- *Sample Trust-Building Plan Template*
- *Steps to an Effective Workplace Apology*
- *Checklist for Transparent Communication Practices*

(See Appendix A: Workplace Restoration Toolkit to restore trust today.)

Prayer for Restoring Trust in the Workplace

Heavenly Father,

You are the God of restoration, the One who keeps every promise, whose Word is flawless, and whose love is unwavering. In a world where trust is too often broken, we look to You, our firm foundation, to teach us how to build again.

Lord, we confess that we have not always been trustworthy in our workplaces. We have sometimes spoken when we should have listened, assumed when we should have asked, and led with fear instead of love. Forgive us, Father, for the times we broke confidence, acted without integrity, or chose convenience over courage.

But today, we return, we return to Your way. We ask for the wisdom to walk in consistency, the strength to communicate with truth and love, and the humility to apologize when we fall short.

Father, make us safe spaces for others to heal. Let our words be seasoned with grace, our leadership clothed in compassion, and our actions rooted in faithfulness. Help us rebuild what has been damaged, not with perfection, but with persistence.

Where trust has been lost in our workplace, let Your Spirit begin the healing. Where silence has taken the place of communication, Let Your voice stir hearts back to openness. Where betrayal has lingered, let Your mercy bring freedom and forgiveness.

We declare: *Our workplace is not beyond redemption. You are restoring what's been fractured, rebuilding what's been forgotten, and reviving relationships, teams, and cultures through Your truth and love.*

THE RESTORED WORKPLACE

May we be restorers. May we lead like Jesus with integrity, empathy, and transparency. May our yes be yes, and our no be no. And may the work of our hands be blessed because it is built on trust.

In Jesus' Name we pray, Amen.

CHAPTER 6

Communication that Heals Intead of Hurts

The Power of Words in the Workplace

Words are powerful. They can heal or they can harm. They can build trust or break it. They can restore what's been lost or deepen wounds that were never addressed.

Nowhere is this more evident than in the workplace, where diverse personalities come together, deadlines loom, and expectations often run high. In such environments, communication can quickly shift from constructive to cutting...from connection to conflict.

But if we are serious about restoring our workplaces, about creating cultures marked by collaboration, growth, and God-ordained purpose, then we must become intentional with our words.

We must choose to speak in ways that bring healing, not harm. To lead with language that empowers, not controls. To communicate in ways that unite, not divide.

This kind of communication is not a *soft skill*. It's a leadership skill. It's a Kingdom skill. And in a world of rushed replies, passive-aggressive emails, and filtered conversations, it's needed now more than ever.

What Healing Communication Looks Like

Healing communication doesn't avoid hard conversations; it approaches them with humility and grace. It doesn't sugarcoat the truth, but it also doesn't weaponize it. It creates space for honesty without shame, correction without condemnation, and collaboration without competition.

Healing communication reflects the heart of Christ. It slows down to listen. It chooses clarity over assumption. It asks questions before casting judgment. It speaks life, especially when it would be easier to talk about frustration.

This kind of communication builds bridges instead of walls. It softens defensiveness. It restores dignity. And over time, it transforms teams, relationships, and entire workplace cultures.

Why Healing Communication Matters

Scripture says it plainly in Proverbs 18:21, AMP: "Death and life are in the power of the tongue, and those who love it and indulge it will eat its fruit and bear the consequences of their words."

Every word we speak carries the potential to either breathe life into relationships or quietly drain the life from them.

In today's fast-paced, often stress-filled workplaces, communicating can make the difference between building a thriving, unified team or fostering a culture of silent resentment and division.

Healthy communication fosters empathy, strengthens trust, defuses conflicts before they escalate, boosts morale, creates psychological safety, and multiplies collaboration and loyalty.

On the other hand, broken communication, careless words, poor listening, avoidance, and harshness create assumptions, breed fear, erode trust, fracture teams, and eventually destroy cultures from the inside out.

In workplaces where communication heals, relationships thrive, and dreams are protected. In workplaces where communication hurts, hearts wither and destinies are delayed.

How Communication Hurts and How to Heal It

Healing communication begins when we recognize the subtle ways communication can wound and intentionally choose a better, higher way.

Poor listening: When we listen only to reply instead of listening to truly understand, we create emotional distance. Healing communication requires active listening, focusing entirely, asking clarifying questions, and validating what the speaker is sharing.

Biblical Wisdom: "Understand this, my beloved brothers and sisters. Let everyone be quick to hear [be a careful, thoughtful listener], slow to speak [a speaker of carefully chosen words and], slow to anger [patient, reflective, forgiving];" (James 1:19, AMP).

Empowerment Strategy: Practice mirroring, repeating back what someone says before offering your thoughts. "What I'm hearing you say is... Did I get that right?"

Harsh or Careless Words: Words spoken in anger, sarcasm, or impatience wound the spirit and destroy trust. Healing communication speaks the truth, but always cloaks it in grace, respect, and compassion.

Biblical Wisdom: "Pleasant words are like a honeycomb, sweet and delightful to the soul and healing to the body." Proverbs 16:24, AMP.

Empowerment Strategy: Before speaking, pause and ask yourself, "Is this kind? Is this clear? Is this necessary?" If not, reshape your words or hold them back.

Withholding Communication: Silence, avoidance, and lack of feedback are forms of unhealthy communication that quietly rot relationships. Healing workplaces normalize courageous, loving conversations, even when they are uncomfortable.

Biblical Wisdom: Speak the truth in love. "But speaking the truth in love [in all things—both our speech and our lives expressing His truth], let us grow up in all things into Him [following His example] who is the Head—Christ.." (Ephesians 4:15, AMP).

Empowerment Strategy: Create regular feedback loops and check-ins, ensuring open dialogue is expected, safe, and valued.

Reactive vs. Responsive Communication: When emotions run high, it's easy to react impulsively, and reactions often inflame rather than heal. Healing communication chooses response over reaction, rooted in patience and prayerful self-control.

Biblical Wisdom: "A soft and gentle and thoughtful answer turns away wrath, But harsh and painful and careless words stir up anger." (Proverbs 15:1, AMP).

Empowerment Strategy: Pause before responding to emotionally charged comments. Breathe, pray internally, and choose words that heal rather than harm.

Creating a Culture of Communication That Heals

Healing communication doesn't just happen one-on-one. It must become a cultural value, embedded into the very DNA of the workplace.

1. Prioritize Empathy

Train yourself and your teams to feel with others, not just think about them. Empathy doesn't require agreement, only understanding.

Practical Step: In every difficult conversation, first validate the emotions before jumping to problem-solving. "I can see why that would feel frustrating. Let's work through it together."

2. Practice Active Listening

Use your body language, eye contact, and silence to show people they are heard. Repeat back what you hear to ensure proper understanding.

3. Foster Open Dialogue

Create environments where every voice, regardless of rank, is honored and invited. Innovation thrives when honesty and ideas are welcomed.

4. Deliver Messages with Care and Respect

Even when feedback is tough, deliver it with love. Hard

truths, spoken in tenderness, lead to breakthrough.

5. Cultivate Psychological Safety

Psychological safety means people feel free to speak, take risks, fail, and grow without fear of retaliation or ridicule.

Practical Step: Publicly celebrate when someone shows courageous honesty by admitting a mistake, offering feedback, or asking a vulnerable question.

6. Build Trust Gradually Through Communication

Trust is built not in grand declarations, but in daily conversations, small, steady moments of honesty, empathy, and consistency.

Healing Communication Changes Everything

When communication heals instead of hurts, the entire atmosphere of the workplace transforms. Teams become families. Leaders become shepherds. Conflict becomes a catalyst for growth rather than a source of division. Purpose reignites, and trust deepens.

Most importantly, the workplace begins to reflect the Kingdom of God, where truth and love work hand-in-hand, where unity is treasured, and where destinies are unleashed instead of delayed.

Healing communication isn't just about what you say. It's about how you say it, why you say it, and whose heart you are protecting as you say it. When we choose to speak with wisdom, patience, and love, we become builders of bridges, not barriers, in the places God has assigned us.

Practical Habits of Restorative Communicators

Healing communication doesn't just happen; it's cultivated through intentional habits practiced daily. Here are some that matter most:

1. **Pause Before You Respond**: Take a moment to breathe, pray, or reflect before reacting. A pause can be the difference between wounding and wisdom.

"Everyone should be quick to listen, slow to speak, and slow to become angry." (James 1:19).

2. **Listen to Understand, Not Just to Reply**: Active listening is a form of respect. It says, "I care enough to hear you fully before I speak."

3. **Speak the Truth in Love**: Truth without love can harm. Love without truth can mislead. Healing communication carries both.

"Speak the truth in love, growing in every way more and more like Christ." (Ephesians 4:15).

4. **Use Words that Restore, Not Diminish**: Choose language that uplifts, encourages, and corrects with compassion. Words carry spiritual weight, use them wisely.

"Gracious words are a honeycomb, sweet to the soul and healing to the bones." (Proverbs 16:24).

5. **Clarify Instead of Assuming**: Misunderstandings

multiply when we don't ask questions. If something feels off, get curious, not critical.

6. Offer Timely Encouragement: Don't wait for a performance review or a crisis to affirm someone. A well-timed word of encouragement can shift an entire day or a career.

7. Apologize and Repair When You Miss It: Even the best communicators get it wrong. Healing begins when we take ownership, offer a sincere apology, and make amends.

Reflection Questions

Pause and reflect:

1. When have I seen communication heal or hurt a workplace I've been part of?
2. In what situations am I tempted to react instead of respond with wisdom?
3. How can I model healing communication with my coworkers, leaders, or team today?

Workplace Healing Action Step

Here are a few ways to put healing communication into action this week:

- Practice active listening during your next one-on-one or team meeting. Reflect on what you hear before offering your input.
- Identify one relationship at work that could benefit from a healing conversation, and prayerfully prepare to take the first step.
- Send an encouraging email or message to someone

who has recently demonstrated courage, creativity, or honesty.

Destiny Declarations

Speak these life-giving words aloud over yourself and your workplace:

- *My words bring healing, hope, and unity wherever I go.*
- *I listen with love, speak with wisdom, and lead with grace.*
- *Through Christ, my communication builds bridges, not barriers.*

Workplace Restoration Toolkit (Appendix Reference)

Find practical tools to deepen healing communication in the Appendix:

- **Healing Conversation Starters for Teams**
- **Self-Assessment: How Healing Are My Words?**
- **Script Templates for Giving and Receiving Feedback with Grace**

(See Appendix A: Workplace Restoration Toolkit for ready-to-use resources.

Prayer for Healing Communication in the Workplace

Heavenly Father,

Thank You for the gift of words, for the divine ability to speak life, encouragement, and healing into the world around us. Today, I ask You to sanctify my mouth, soften my heart, and sharpen my awareness of how my communication affects others.

In moments of pressure, help me pause and reflect before I respond. May my words be seasoned with grace, truth, and patience. When I'm tempted to speak from frustration or fear, help me choose compassion and clarity instead.

Lord, I confess the times I've allowed careless speech, silence, or sarcasm to wound the very people I'm called to walk alongside. I release that guilt to You now and receive Your forgiveness and restoration.

Make me a vessel of Your peace in every meeting, message, and moment. Teach me to listen with my whole heart, not just to reply but to understand. Let empathy lead my language. Let humility guide my tone. Let love be the filter for every complicated conversation.

Father, transform our workplace into an atmosphere of trust, safety, and collaboration where truth is spoken in love, feedback is offered with kindness, and communication builds bridges instead of barriers.

Help me model this kind of healing communication, even when it's not easy or reciprocated. Make me bold in honesty, gentle in correction, and joyful in encouragement.

I declare that my words will not be weapons, but tools of restoration. My communication will not spark division, but invite unity. And that, through You, I will become a Restorer in every room I enter.

In Jesus' Name, Amen.

CHAPTER 7

Psychological Safety:
The New Superpower of Organizations

Psychological Safety: The Hidden Superpower of Thriving Teams

In today's fast-paced, ever-changing workplaces, one factor quietly determines whether teams will merely survive or truly thrive: *Psychological safety.*

It's the hidden superpower of healthy, high-functioning teams. The invisible atmosphere that either invites people to bring their whole selves or pressures them to shrink back and stay silent.

Psychological safety means creating an environment where people feel secure enough to:

- Speak honestly without fear.
- Ask questions without shame.
- Share ideas without being dismissed.
- Admit mistakes without retaliation.
- Offer feedback and even disagreement, with respect and without punishment.

This is not a luxury or a *"nice-to-have"* for forward-thinking companies. It's a necessity, especially for those who want to build cultures marked by creativity, collaboration, innovation, excellence, and lasting Kingdom impact.

Where psychological safety is missing, potential quietly withers. People become cautious, disengaged, and emotionally guarded. They hold back not just ideas, but their God-given brilliance, compassion, and calling.

But where psychological safety is present, people begin to breathe. They show up with courage. They speak with clarity. They lead with heart. And in that kind of environment, destinies flourish, and dreams come alive.

Why Psychological Safety Is So Critical Today

Modern workplaces are facing unprecedented challenges. In-person teams present their own challenges. However, remote and hybrid teams can make communication trickier and genuine connections harder. Diverse teams bring extraordinary strength but also greater potential for misunderstandings if trust and empathy are not intentionally cultivated.

Stress, anxiety, and burnout have reached historic highs across nearly every industry. Employees, especially the rising generations, are no longer satisfied with just a paycheck. They seek meaning, belonging, authenticity, and purpose in their work.

Without psychological safety, teams devolve into survival mode. Employees stay silent about risks, problems, and even brilliant ideas. Conflict festers underground instead of being addressed with honesty and compassion. Innovation dies quietly because no one feels safe enough to risk "failing forward." Morale plummets as individuals begin to feel unseen, unheard, and unvalued.

Jesus said plainly in Mark 3:25: "If a house is divided against itself, that house cannot stand." A workplace without psychological safety is a divided house, unstable, untrusting, and ultimately unsustainable.

Psychological Safety: Safe vs. Unsafe Workplaces

In a *psychologically safe workplace*, people feel free to ask questions without fear of looking incompetent. Mistakes are seen as learning opportunities rather than failures to be punished. Team members are encouraged to give and receive feedback with honesty and grace, knowing it will be met with respect, not defensiveness.

Disagreements aren't viewed as threats; they're welcomed as part of healthy dialogue that leads to better outcomes. Leaders in these environments model vulnerability and transparency, fostering a culture where authenticity is valued more highly than image.

Everyone's voice is valued, not just the loudest or most senior in the room. Trust is built through consistent actions, clear communication, and genuine care. The result? People feel energized, connected, and motivated. Innovation thrives because individuals are free to share bold ideas without fear of rejection. Collaboration flows naturally, and the overall atmosphere becomes one of hope, healing, and shared purpose.

In contrast, *a psychologically unsafe workplace* breeds silence and caution. Team members hold back questions and concerns, fearing they'll be judged or dismissed. Mistakes are hidden rather than admitted, because the cost of vulnerability feels too high.

Feedback is avoided altogether, or when given, it's taken as a personal attack rather than a gift for growth. Disagreements are often perceived as insubordination, and individuals who challenge the status quo are frequently sidelined.

Leaders in unsafe environments tend to protect their image rather than share their struggles, creating a culture of pretense and guardedness. Only a select few voices are heard, usually those deemed "safe". Micromanagement, inconsistency, or passive-aggressive leadership erodes trust. The result is a culture marked by tension, burnout, and emotional disconnection. Innovation stalls, collaboration declines, and people begin to emotionally check out long before they ever leave the building.

Real Challenges Employers and Employees Are Facing

Today's workplaces are grappling with real barriers that prevent psychological safety from flourishing:

- **Fear of Speaking Up:** Employees often worry that offering feedback, admitting a mistake, or proposing a new idea could cost them their reputation, relationships, or even their jobs.
- **Micromanagement:** Leaders operating from fear or insecurity hover over every task, sending the unspoken message that trust is absent and mistakes are unacceptable.
- **Bias and Exclusion:** When biases and favoritism go unaddressed, certain voices are valued over others, creating quiet barriers of resentment and discouragement.
- **Shaming Mistakes:** Some workplaces treat mistakes as permanent failures rather than growth opportunities, causing employees to hide errors instead of learning from them.
- **Poor or Inconsistent Feedback:** Without regular, constructive feedback, employees feel anxious, confused, and isolated, never quite sure where they stand.

These challenges are not small. But the good news is: with intention, courage, and Christ-centered leadership, they can be overcome.

Biblical Wisdom for Creating Safe, Thriving Workplaces

The Bible gives us powerful guidance for building environments where safety, growth, and trust thrive:

1. Encourage, Don't Tear Down:

Therefore encourage and comfort one another and build up one another, just as you are doing. — *1 Thessalonians 5:11, AMP*

2. Correct with Grace:

Brethren, if a man is overtaken in any trespass, you who are spiritual restore such a one in a spirit of gentleness, considering yourself lest you also be tempted. — *Galatians 6:1, NKJV*

3. Value Every Voice:

There is neither Jew nor Greek, slave nor free, male nor female, for you are all one in Christ Jesus. — *Galatians 3:28, NIV*

4. Model Servant Leadership:

Whoever wants to become great among you must be your servant. — *Matthew 20:26, NIV*

God's wisdom, the Kingdom way, is not about control, fear, or dominance. It is about honor, humility, and restoration.

How to Foster Psychological Safety

Healing workplace culture through psychological safety

doesn't happen by accident. It happens through intentional, daily actions.

1. Prioritize Clear, Caring Communication

Feedback should be regular, respectful, and two-way. Communicate, not just decisions, but the heart and reasoning behind them.

Empowerment Strategy: Set team norms like "assume positive intent" and "seek clarity, not conflict" to create a safe foundation for every conversation.

2. Build Trust Through Accountability

Hold everyone, especially leaders, accountable for treating others with dignity, honesty, and compassion. Accountability without condemnation builds lasting safety.

Empowerment Strategy: Make it crystal clear that toxic behavior (gossip, bullying, exclusion) will not be tolerated, regardless of someone's title or tenure.

3. Encourage Open Dialogue

Make it not only safe but expected that team members offer ideas, share feedback, and raise concerns. Reward courageous communication.

Empowerment Strategy: End meetings by asking, "Whose voice haven't we heard yet?" and make intentional space for everyone.

4. Embrace Vulnerability

Leaders must first model vulnerability, admitting when they don't know something, have made a mistake, or need help.

Biblical Wisdom: My grace is sufficient for you, for my power is made perfect in weakness.

My grace is sufficient for you {My lovingkindness and My mercy are more than enough—always available—regardless of the situation}; for {My} power is being perfected {and is completed and shows itself most effectively} in {your} weakness." Therefore, I will all the more gladly boast in my weaknesses, so that the power of Christ {may completely enfold me and} may dwell in me.
— 2 Corinthians 12:9, AMP.

5. Model Curiosity Instead of Judgment

Replace assumptions with questions. When you disagree, lean in with curiosity instead of pulling away in offense.

Empowerment Strategy: Practice saying, "Help me understand your perspective."

6. Create an Environment Where Mistakes Are Learning Opportunities

Normalize the idea that mistakes are not fatal; they are feedback that fuels growth.

Practical Step: Host "lessons learned" debriefs after projects, where mistakes are analyzed with gratitude, not shame.

7. Practice Inclusive Decision-Making

Involve a variety of voices when making important decisions. Honor the wisdom of different backgrounds, experiences, and insights.

Biblical Wisdom: *Plans fail for lack of counsel, but with many advisers they succeed.* — *Proverbs 15:22, NIV*

8. Provide Consistent Feedback and Recognition

Feedback should be frequent, honest, and aimed at growth. Recognition should celebrate not just outcomes but courage, collaboration, and creativity.

9. Foster a True Culture of Belonging

Go beyond diversity to cultivate true belonging, where every individual feels celebrated because of who they are, not despite it.

Healing Workplace Culture Through Psychological Safety

When psychological safety is present, everything shifts. People feel free to be creative, to collaborate authentically, and to take healthy risks.

Innovation multiplies because fear diminishes. Teams become resilient because mistakes are embraced as stepping stones, not stigmas.

Relationships strengthen because communication flows honestly and honorably. Psychological safety transforms a workplace from a battlefield into a garden, where purpose is planted, dreams are nurtured, and destinies bloom.

How to Cultivate Psychological Safety (Action List)

These simple, intentional practices help leaders and teams create emotionally safe environments where people can thrive:

1. Model Vulnerability First: Share your own challenges, doubts, or failures with humility. When leaders go first, it gives others permission to be honest too.

2. Respond with Curiosity, Not Judgment: When someone brings feedback, an idea, or even a mistake, pause and ask questions instead of reacting defensively. Seek to understand before correcting.

3. Welcome All Voices to the Table: Make space for every team member to contribute, especially those who may be quieter or often overlooked. Invite input regularly, and listen.

4. Normalize Learning Moments: Celebrate progress, not just perfection. When someone admits a mistake, affirm their courage before addressing the correction.

5. Establish Clear Boundaries and Expectations: Clarity reduces anxiety. Let your team know what's okay, what's not, and how feedback will be received. Safety grows in structured freedom.

6. Uplift in Public, Correct in Private: Public affirmation builds trust; public embarrassment erodes it. Handle correction with care and dignity.

7. Reward Honesty, Not Just Results: Let people

know that character matters as much as performance. Praise integrity, humility, and courage just as much as outcomes.

Reflection Questions

Take a moment to reflect:

1. On a scale of 1 to 10, how safe do I feel to speak openly and honestly at work?
2. Where can I model vulnerability and curiosity more intentionally in my leadership or interactions?
3. What is one action I can take this week to help someone else feel safer sharing, leading, or growing?

Workplace Healing Action Steps

Choose one or more of these steps to put healing into action:

- Openly thank someone who showed courage, whether they spoke up, admitted a mistake, or offered a new idea.
- Host a *"Lessons Learned"* conversation after a meeting or project, focusing on successes and growth areas.
- Personally ask a team member for feedback on how you could create a safer environment for them.

Destiny Declarations

Speak these faith-filled declarations aloud:

- *I create spaces where others feel seen, heard, and valued.*
- *Through Christ, I foster courage, creativity, and collabo-*

ration wherever I go.
- *Mistakes are opportunities for growth, not reasons for shame.*

Workplace Restoration Toolkit (Appendix Reference)

In the Appendix, you'll find powerful tools to foster psychological safety today:

- *Psychological Safety Assessment Survey*
- *Sample Scripts for Encouraging Courageous Conversations*
- *Checklist for Creating a Belonging Culture*

(See Appendix A: Workplace Restoration Toolkit for ready-to-use resources.)

Prayer to Make This Workplace Safe and Strong

Heavenly Father,

You are the God of peace, wisdom, and restoration. Today, we come before You with open hearts and surrendered hands, asking You to breathe new life into the places where we work, lead, and serve.

Lord, we acknowledge that true healing in the workplace cannot happen without the presence of safety, psychological safety that reflects Your heart of compassion, truth, and grace. You are the One who sees beyond roles and titles, values every voice, and never silences a cry for help or a word of truth. Teach us to build that same kind of safety in our work environments.

Father, uproot every fear that has taken root in the hearts of teams, fear of judgment, fear of rejection, fear of failure. Tear down the strongholds of silence and suspicion that keep us divided. Where there has been micromanagement, *bring trust;* where there has been bias or exclusion, *plant belonging.* Where mistakes have been met with shame, *pour out grace upon grace.*

Help us become leaders who listen deeply, correct gently, and lift others boldly. Let our feedback be life-giving, not soul-crushing. Let our meetings be moments of connection, not competition. Let our decisions be shaped by wisdom, counsel, and inclusion, not pride or power.

God, give us the courage to model vulnerability: to say, "I don't know," "I was wrong," or "I need help," without shame. Help us lead not from fear but from faith. Let our weakness be the very place where Your strength is revealed.

Where there's been burnout, we speak restoration. Where there's been silence, we declare a safe space for every voice. Where there's been division, we declare unity and purpose. Where there's been anxiety, we release Your peace.

Jesus, You said a house divided cannot stand. So make our workplaces whole: houses of honor, fields of favor, and gardens of growth. Let psychological safety become our culture, not just our concept. Let it be the soil where purpose is planted, talents are watered, and Kingdom impact blooms.

Holy Spirit, convict us quickly and lead us gently. Show us the one step we can take today to create a safer space for someone else. Let us be a light in the breakroom, boardroom, and every Zoom room. May our workplaces become sanctuaries of healing and innovation because You dwell there with us.

We declare it now by faith: *We are restorers of culture, cultivators of courage, and ambassadors of Your Kingdom and Your Way in the workplace.*

In Jesus' Name we pray, Amen.

Part III:
Personal Healing for Collective Transformation

CHAPTER 8

Healing the Heart You Bring to Work

Even the most inspiring workplace culture, full of great policies, visionary leaders, and intentional values, can be quietly undone by *one unhealed heart*. Because pain that goes unaddressed doesn't stay hidden.

It leaks. It leaks into conversations through sarcasm or silence. It shows up in decisions clouded by fear, in relationships strained by mistrust, in leadership shaped more by self-protection than service.

No matter how beautiful a workplace looks on the surface, if the people within it are carrying unhealed wounds, unresolved anger, hidden bitterness, or deep insecurity, that pain will eventually shape the culture, whether we mean for it to or not.

We cannot fully restore our workplaces until we *first tend to the hearts that fill them*, starting with our own. Healing the heart you bring to work isn't just about feeling better. It's not just personal wellness.

It's leadership work. It's Kingdom work. It's destiny work. Because healed hearts don't just show up differently; they lead differently. They listen differently.

They forgive faster. They build safer, stronger, more redemptive spaces for others to thrive. And when workplaces begin to heal, the ripple effect is undeniable.

Families begin to heal. Communities grow stronger. Futures are reshaped...for the better. This isn't just about work. This is about legacy.

Why Personal Healing Matters at Work

Workplaces are not machines made of policies and spreadsheets. They are living, breathing ecosystems of human souls designed by God for connection, creativity, stewardship, and purpose. When we bring wounded hearts to work, we unintentionally sabotage the very environments we are trying to build.

When our hearts carry old pain into new places:

- We react disproportionately to minor conflicts.
- We interpret feedback as personal rejection instead of growth.
- We either withdraw in fear or dominate in insecurity.
- We replicate cycles of mistrust, division, and burnout without realizing it.

Proverbs 4:23, NIV gives us this timeless wisdom: "Above all else, guard your heart, for everything you do flows from it." Everything, meaning our conversations, leadership, collaboration, the condition of our relationships, life experiences, and influence, flows from the condition of our hearts.

Healing your heart isn't just about feeling better. It's about being positioned to lead, build, love, and create in a way that transforms everyone connected to you: your co-workers, teams, family, church, community, and the generations to come.

The Real Wounds People Carry to Work

Many people walking into offices and Zoom meetings

today are carrying invisible, but heavy, wounds:

1. **Workplace-Related Trauma:** Past experiences of harassment, bullying, betrayal, or injustice leave scars that affect trust, communication, and engagement

2. **Unrealistic Expectations:** Cultures that demand constant hustle, perfection, or self-sacrifice erode emotional resilience and fuel quiet resentment.

3. **Boundary Violations:** When workplaces disrespect personal time, dignity, or autonomy, employees carry the silent weight of burnout and bitterness.

4. **Unhealed Childhood or Life Trauma:** Somtimes, workplace frustrations trigger older wounds: feelings of abandonment, inadequacy, or fear rooted far before the first job offer ever came.

Until these wounds are recognized, honored, and healed, they will continue to color how we lead, follow, serve, and dream.

Start with the Heart: Steps and Questions for Personal Healing in the Workplace

Before we can restore what's broken around us, we must be willing to face what's still broken within us. This is not about shame; *it's about freedom.* It's about healing the places that have been quietly carrying pain, fear, or disappointment for far too long.

These questions and steps are designed to help you begin that journey, guided by honesty, grace, and the loving presence of God every step of the way.

Step 1: Identify the Wounds

Ask yourself:

1. Is there a past workplace experience that still stirs anger, anxiety, or sadness when I think about it?
2. Have I been deeply hurt by a leader, coworker, or team dynamic that I never fully processed?
3. Am I still carrying the weight of betrayal, rejection, or burnout from a previous job?

Write it down. Name the wound. You cannot heal what you will not name. God is not afraid of your honesty.

Step 2: Examine the Symptoms

Ask yourself:

1. Do I find it hard to trust others at work, even when they haven't given me a reason not to?
2. Am I overly defensive, overly quiet, or quick to disengage when tension arises?
3. Do I struggle with impostor syndrome, perfectionism, or people-pleasing in professional spaces?

Pay attention to patterns. They often point to places that still need healing, not condemnation, but compassion.

Step 3: Invite God Into the Process

Ask yourself:

1. Have I invited God to heal this part of my story, or have I tried to just "push through"?

2. What might it look like to bring this pain to Him instead of carrying it alone?
3. What does Scripture say about healing, renewal, and transformation in my life?

Pause and pray. Ask the Holy Spirit to show you what's ready to be restored. You don't have to fix it all at once. Start by inviting Him in.

He heals the brokenhearted and binds up their wounds {healing their pain and comforting their sorrow}. —Psalm 147:3, AMP

Step 4: Begin Restoring from the Inside Out

Ask yourself:

1. What one step can I take this week to release resentment or fear?
2. Who do I need to forgive, maybe even myself?
3. How can I speak or lead differently now that I'm aware of what I've been carrying?

Take small, intentional steps. Healing is a process. But with each courageous choice, the heart grows lighter, and the workplace grows stronger.

Final Encouragement: You are not alone in your healing. God is not done with your story. And the pain you've carried does not disqualify you; it equips you to lead with deeper compassion and wisdom.

Solutions: How to Heal the Heart You Bring to Work

Healing is not a one-time event. It is a sacred journey

rooted in intentional practices, empowered mindsets, and deeply rooted in the truth of God's Word and power.

Here's how to begin:

1. Prioritize Deep Self-Care: Not Surface-Level Escapes

Self-care isn't about luxury, it's about stewardship. It's about caring for the vessel that carries your calling. It's about returning to and connecting regularly with the One who created you for and gave you your life calling.

Healing Practices:

- Daily prayer and Scripture meditation (Psalm 1:2)
- Journaling to process emotions honestly before God
- Seeking therapy or Christian counseling if needed
- Caring for your body with sleep, nutrition, and movement
- Honoring Sabbath rhythms and sacred rest

Begin to implement intentional patterns of rest, renewal, and reconnection with God that are woven into daily, weekly, and seasonal life, not just a single day off. Patterns and rhythms rooted in God's own rhythm of work and rest in creation (Genesis 2:2–3). These are commanded (as a gift) for His people (Exodus 20:8–11).

2. Recognize and Address Workplace-Related Trauma

Healing begins with truth. Be honest about the wounds you carry from past jobs, toxic leaders, or unsafe teams.

Healing Practices:

- Name the wounds prayerfully before God (Psalm 147:3).
- Seek wise counsel to help process pain.
- Forgive, even when you remember, to release your own soul from bondage (Matthew 6:14-15).

3. Establish Clear Boundaries

Boundaries are not barriers to love but bridges to healthy, sustainable service.

Healing Practices:

- Define work hours and protect them.
- Clarify workload limits and expectations.
- Say "no" respectfully when needed.
- Refuse to internalize every problem as your personal burden.

Biblical Wisdom:

Let your yes be yes and your no be no. — Matthew 5:37

4. Cultivate Empathy, Starting with Yourself

Many of us extend grace to others, but starve ourselves of it.

Healing Practices:

- Replace harsh self-talk with truth: *"God loves me and I am enough in Christ."*
- Celebrate progress, not just perfection.
- See your limits not as flaws but as invitations to rely

on God's strength.

5. Embrace Healing Practices at Work

Small daily choices create massive heart transformation over time. Make sure the daily choices are positive so that your heart, and therefore, your life, business, and career are moving in a positive direction.

Healing Practices:

- Take 60 seconds of deep breathing before tense meetings.
- Pray silently over projects, clients, or conflicts.
- Speak blessings (even silently) over coworkers who challenge you.
- End each day by listing three things you're grateful for.

6. Create a Personal Support System

Healing happens faster and deeper in community.

Healing Practices:

- Surround yourself with people who pray for you, speak truth to you, and celebrate your growth.
- Pursue mentors who model emotional and spiritual wholeness.
- Lean into godly community, small groups, church families, and prayer circles.

Biblical Wisdom:

Two are better than one, because they have a good return for their labor: If either of them falls down, one can help the other up. But pity anyone who falls and has no one to help them up.
— Ecclesiastes 4:9-10, NIV.

7. Reconnect to Your Sense of Purpose

Purpose is your anchor when work gets heavy or discouraging. It reminds you that your value is not rooted in applause, relationships, or achievements but in assignment.

Healing Practices:

- Write a simple personal mission statement.
- Reflect often on who you are serving and why.
- Pray daily: "Lord, help me to work as unto You, not for human masters." (Colossians 3:23)

Biblical Wisdom:

Whatever you do {whatever your task may be}, work from the soul {that is, put in your very best effort}, as {something done} for the Lord and not for men. — Colossians 3:23, AMP

What a Healed Heart Brings to the Workplace

When you carry a healed heart into your workplace, you take God's Kingdom with you. You will bring:

- **Patience** instead of panic
- **Kindness** instead of criticism
- **Courage** instead of cowardice
- **Creativity** instead of competition
- **Collaboration** instead of control

- **Faith** instead of fear

Healing your heart means walking into every meeting, conversation, and challenge with the peace, wisdom, and strength of Christ. And without even realizing it, you will create ripples of restoration that change the culture around you.

Reflection Questions

Take time with the Lord to reflect honestly:

1. What workplace or life wounds am I still carrying into my current role?
2. Where do I need to set stronger emotional or practical boundaries?
3. What healing rhythms or consistent actions can I incorporate into my daily life starting today?

Workplace Healing Action Steps

Here are simple but powerful steps you can take this week:

- Set one new healthy boundary, and communicate it with clarity and grace.
- Spend five quiet minutes journaling a prayer asking God to reveal hidden wounds still needing healing.
- Choose one daily healing practice, such as a prayer break, gratitude journal, or breathing exercise, and commit to it for 30 days.

Destiny Declarations

Speak these truth-filled declarations over your life:

- *Through Christ, my heart is healed, whole, and hopeful.*
- *I am bringing healing, not hurt, into every space I enter.*
- *I steward my heart wisely to fulfill God's plan and my Kingdom assignment with excellence and joy.*

Workplace Restoration Toolkit (Appendix Reference)

To support your healing journey, you'll find these practical tools in the Appendix:

- *Personal Heart-Check Reflection Worksheet*
- *Boundary-Setting Scripts for Difficult Conversations*
- *Self-Care and Healing Routine Planner*

(See Appendix A: Workplace Restoration Toolkit for exercises you can start today.)

Prayer: Lord, Heal the Heart I Bring to Work

Heavenly Father,

You are the Healer of the brokenhearted, the Restorer of souls, and the Keeper of our purpose. Today, I come before You with honest hands and a willing heart, asking You to search me, heal me, and prepare me to carry Your love and light into every space I enter, including my workplace.

God, I acknowledge the truth: I've brought wounds to work. Some are fresh. Others are hidden, buried deep beneath years of silence, perfectionism, or pressure. But You see them all. And You love me still.

So I invite You now to come into the places I've kept guarded. Touch the pain I've tucked away behind my title, to-do list, and brave face. Heal the disappointments, the betrayals, the burnout, the moments I felt unseen, unheard, or unworthy. Let Your love be the balm that soothes the aching parts of my story.

Lord, forgive me for the times I let my unhealed places bleed onto others. For when I reacted instead of responded… withheld instead of embraced… controlled instead of trusted. I lay those patterns down now at Your feet.

Jesus, guard my heart as Your Word commands because I now understand that everything I do flows from it. So create in me a clean heart, O God, and renew a right spirit within me. Make me whole, not just for my sake, but for every soul I will encounter in meetings, emails, hallways, and challenging conversations.

Teach me how to set healthy boundaries without guilt. Help me care for my mind and body without shame. Let me see rest not as weakness but as worship. And when old triggers arise, remind me to pause, breathe, and lean into Your grace.

Surround me with wise counsel, with people who speak truth in love and lift me when I forget who I am. Reignite my purpose, Lord: let me work not for applause, but out of assignment. Let every task, every effort, and every interaction reflect You.

Father, may my healing become someone else's hope. Let the heart I bring to work be a living testimony that You still restore, that You still transform, that You still use ordinary people to carry out extraordinary Kingdom work.

I declare today: I am healed. I am whole. I am bringing light, not pain, peace, not pressure, purpose, not performance.

In the mighty Name of Jesus, Amen.

CHAPTER 9

Forgiveness:
The Leadership Advantage Nobody Talks About

Forgiveness: The Secret Weapon of Restored Leadership

Forgiveness may be one of the most powerful leadership tools we have, yet it's rarely talked about in the workplace.

Why? Because in a world that runs on deadlines, performance, and competition, forgiveness can feel risky, unproductive, and maybe even naive.

But here's the truth: forgiveness is not weakness; it's wisdom. It's not passive; it's powerful. And it's one of the boldest choices any leader or team member can make.

You don't have to look far to see what happens when forgiveness is withheld. Resentment simmers under the surface. Tension grows. Good people shut down, give up, or quietly walk away. Even the most talented teams get stuck because no one's willing to let go of the offense that's holding everything back. But *when forgiveness enters the room, everything begins to shift.*

Forgiveness can begin the journey to rebuild trust where betrayal once stood. It clears emotional clutter, allowing creativity to flow again. It makes room for honest conversations, new beginnings, and healed relationships.

Forgiveness isn't just a spiritual principle. It's a leadership strategy for building teams that last. It's a Kingdom mindset that turns bitterness into breakthrough.

When leaders and employees choose forgiveness, especially when it's hard, they create a culture where people feel safe to heal, free to grow, and empowered to bring their whole, restored selves to the table.

In a world that shouts about punishment, cancellation, and perfection, forgiveness whispers a better way: redemption, restoration, and renewal. And those are the foundations of any workplace that truly thrives.

Why Forgiveness Matters in the Workplace

Every workplace is made up of imperfect people. Mistakes will happen, misunderstandings will arise, and disappointments will occur. The question isn't *if* conflict will happen; it's how we will respond when it does.

Without forgiveness:

- Grudges fester silently under the surface.
- Conflict escalates unnecessarily.
- Trust erodes faster than it can be rebuilt.
- Talented, purpose-driven employees quietly leave in search of safer ground.

But when forgiveness becomes part of the culture:

- Healing conversations happen sooner.
- Lessons are learned with grace instead of shame.
- Trust grows stronger and more resilient.
- Teams evolve into families, and families build legacies.

The Bible gives us this anchor in Ephesians 4:32, NKJV: "Be kind to one another, tenderhearted, forgiving one another, as God in Christ forgave you." Forgiveness is not optional for those who desire to lead with wisdom and have Kingdom impact. It is essential, and the lifeblood of cultures that thrive.

What Happens When Forgiveness Is Missing

Where forgiveness is absent, resentment moves in and quietly suffocates the life out of organizations. Minor offenses turn into major relational rifts.

Creativity dries up because no one feels safe enough to risk being wrong. Employees become guarded, defensive, and emotionally detached. Leadership credibility crumbles under the weight of hypocrisy and double standards.

The silent killer of morale and mission is often not incompetence; it's *unresolved resentment*. Forgiveness doesn't excuse irresponsibility. It redeems brokenness so that learning, trust, and unity can be restored. Forgiveness is not about ignoring wrongs. It's about refusing to allow wrongs to define the future.

How Forgiveness Unlocks Leadership and Team Potential

Forgiveness, when practiced intentionally, creates tangible, measurable advantages for leaders, teams, and entire organizations:

1. **It Fosters Trust:** When people know that mistakes are treated as opportunities for growth, not automatic punishments, they become braver, bolder, and more innovative.
2. **It Encourages Accountability:** Forgiveness doesn't erase consequences, but opens the door for honest ownership. Leaders who model forgiveness create

safe spaces where employees can admit mistakes without fear of humiliation.

3. **It Promotes Growth:** People grow faster and deeper when they are not afraid of being discarded after a failure. Forgiveness creates an atmosphere where stretching and stumbling are honored parts of the journey.

4. **It Strengthens Relationships:** When forgiveness is normal, not rare, workplace relationships become resilient; able to weather challenges without collapsing.

5. **It Multiplies Impact:** Forgiving environments naturally attract top talent. People want to work where grace, not fear, defines the culture.

Biblical Wisdom confirms it beautifully: "Above all, love each other deeply, because love covers over a multitude of sins." (1 Peter 4:8).

Biblical Wisdom:

Above all, have fervent and unfailing love for one another, because love covers a multitude of sins {it overlooks unkindness and unselfishly seeks the best for others}. — 1 Peter 4:8, AMP

How to Walk Through Forgiveness as a Leader or Team Member

Forgiveness is a process, and it often starts with a single, courageous step. Whether you're leading a team or healing from a painful moment at work, here's a practical guide to help you move forward:

1. Acknowledge the Hurt Honestly

Ask yourself: What exactly happened? What was said or done that hurt me? Be honest about how it affected you emotionally, relationally, and even spiritually.

2. Bring It to God First

Pray through the offense. Ask God to help you process it through His lens, not just your pain. Invite the Holy Spirit to reveal anything you might need to release, even if you're still waiting on an apology.

And forgive us our debts, as we have forgiven our debtors {letting go of both the wrong and the resentment}. —Matthew 6:12, AMP

3. Choose to Forgive (Even Before They Apologize)

Forgiveness is not a feeling; it's a decision. Say it aloud or write it down: "I choose to forgive [Name] for [Action]. I release them, and entrust this to God."

4. Set Boundaries if Needed

Forgiveness doesn't mean tolerating toxic behavior or excusing injustice. Determine what healthy boundaries look like moving forward, and communicate them with clarity and grace.

5. Take the Next Step Toward Restoration

If appropriate, have a conversation with the person. Be honest, not harsh. Focus on impact, not accusation. If a conversation isn't possible, focus on changing your posture toward them (through prayer, empathy, or blessing them privately).

6. Lead by Example

If you're a leader, your posture sets the tone for your team. Apologize when needed. Be the first to extend grace. Model what it looks like to repair trust, not just demand it.

7. Repeat as Needed

Forgiveness is often layered. When the pain resurfaces, choose again. Keep releasing. Keep healing. Each time you forgive, your heart grows lighter, and your leadership grows stronger.

Encouragement: Forgiveness at work may feel radical, but it's also redemptive. You don't have to carry the offense any longer. You have the power to lead differently, starting today.

How to Foster Forgiveness in the Workplace

Forgiveness doesn't happen by accident; it must be intentionally modeled, encouraged, and normalized through daily choices:

1. **Prioritize Open Communication:** Create spaces for honest conversations, both structured and informal. Address conflicts early, when they are small and manageable.

Empowerment Strategy: Equip your team with conflict resolution tools and teach them how to bring up offenses respectfully and biblically.

Practice Empathy: Before reacting to mistakes, ask yourself, "What unseen battle might they be fighting?"

Most mistakes come from pressure, miscommunication, or pain, not evil intent.

Healing Practice: Ask: "What else might be happening here that I can't see?"

2. **Encourage Conflict Resolution Training:** Don't fear conflict, train for it. Teach teams how to address offense quickly and with biblical wisdom.

Biblical Blueprint:

If your brother sins, go and show him his fault in private; if he listens and pays attention to you, you have won back your brother.
— *Matthew 18:15, AMP.*

If a fellow believer hurts you, go and tell him—work it out between the two of you. If he listens, you've made a friend.
— *Matthew 18:15, MSG.*

3. **Create Safe Spaces for Expressing Feelings:** When people know they can speak openly about frustrations or hurts without retaliation, forgiveness becomes easier and faster.

Model Forgiveness as a Leader: Leaders set the emotional thermostat. If you model humility, compassion, and forgiveness, your teams will rise to meet you there.

Healing Practice: Apologize when necessary. Forgive generously. Let grace set the tone.

4. **Set Clear Boundaries Around Behavior:** Forgiveness does not mean tolerating repeated toxicity. It's possible to

forgive and still establish firm, kind boundaries that protect the team.

5. Celebrate Stories of Restoration: When conflict is resolved, celebrate it. Let healing, not hurt, become the story your culture tells.

Practical Forgiveness Practices for Individuals and Teams

Healing forgiveness isn't just theoretical; it's practical and powerful.

1. **Daily Heart Check:** Each morning, ask God, "Is there anyone I need to forgive today?" (Mark 11:25)
2. **Conflict Resolution Frameworks:** Use clear, simple steps to resolve offenses quickly and constructively (see *Toolkit exercises*).
3. **Forgiveness Pacts:** Create a team agreement that says, "We commit to forgiving quickly and addressing conflict early."
4. **Prayer Covering:** Encourage praying for each other. It's hard to resent someone you pray blessings over.

The Transforming Power of Forgiveness at Work

Forgiveness may be one of the most overlooked tools in today's workplace, but it's also one of the most powerful. In cultures driven by performance, pressure, and perfectionism, forgiveness can seem countercultural, even naive. But make no mistake: forgiveness is not weakness. It is wisdom.

It is leadership at its highest and most transformative level. Forgiveness is the secret weapon of Restorers, those who choose to lead with heart, humility, and healing.

In workplaces where forgiveness is present, relationships are mended. Trust is rebuilt. Creativity flows again. Teams begin to breathe again. And destinies once delayed by bitterness, resentment, or fear are unlocked.

What Forgiveness Looks Like at Work

Forgiveness in the workplace doesn't always look like a dramatic reconciliation or a tearful apology. Most of the time, it's quiet. Subtle. Intentional. But its impact runs deep.

Here's what forgiveness often really looks like on a daily basis:

- Choosing not to rehearse the offense in your mind, or rehash it with others
- Responding with grace instead of sarcasm, silence, or passive aggression
- Addressing conflict directly and respectfully, rather than avoiding it out of fear
- Giving others the benefit of the doubt, even when you could assume the worst
- Letting go of the need to "win" or be right to move forward
- Releasing the expectation that the person who hurt you must fix it all first
- Making space for restoration, even when full reconciliation may never happen

Forgiveness doesn't excuse the wrong. It doesn't minimize what happened. What it does is free your heart from the grip of that wrong. It releases the offense so that it no longer controls your thoughts, your emotions, or your leadership.

In a world where offenses are often rehearsed, recycled, and rewarded, forgiveness whispers a better way, a Kingdom way. It becomes the spiritual and emotional oxygen that allows people to breathe again, and teams to flourish and prosper again.

What a Forgiving Workplace Looks Like

When forgiveness becomes part of the culture, not just an isolated act, everything begins to change.

In a forgiving workplace:

- People take risks without fear of ridicule or retaliation.
- Teams bounce back more quickly from mistakes and setbacks.
- Leaders gain genuine respect by showing humility and accountability.
- Loyalty runs deeper than fear ever could.
- Innovation and trust flourish beyond what metrics or performance reviews could ever measure.

Forgiveness doesn't erase consequences, but it transforms them. It turns wounds into wisdom. It turns tension into teamwork. It turns past pain into present momentum. Where bitterness once delayed progress, forgiveness accelerates destiny.

Reflection Questions

1. Where am I still holding onto unforgiveness toward a coworker, leader, or employee?

2. How would my workplace transform if forgiveness became the normal culture, not the rare exception?

3. What small act of forgiveness can I practice today to start creating that transformation?

Workplace Healing Action Step

1. Identify one offense, big or small, you are ready to forgive.

2. Pray about it. Release it. If appropriate, engage in a healing conversation.

3. Share a short story with your team about a time when forgiveness led to unexpected restoration.

4. Suggest hosting a *"Forgiveness and Conflict Resolution"* workshop or small group in your workplace.

Final Encouragement

Forgiveness may feel like a personal decision, but in the workplace, it's a culture-shaping force. It creates safety. It restores dignity. It paves the way for trust, creativity, and God-ordained impact.

You don't have to carry that offense any longer. You have the power to release it and, by doing so, to lead with greater clarity, compassion, and freedom. Forgiveness isn't just about healing your past. It's about clearing the way for everything God wants to do next, both in you and in your business or organization.

Destiny Declarations

Speak these life-giving words aloud in faith:
- *I am a carrier of forgiveness, grace, and hope in every environment I enter.*

- *Through Christ, I forgive freely, lead courageously, and restore relationships boldly.*
- *Where I sow forgiveness, God multiplies unity, strength, and purpose.*

Workplace Restoration Toolkit (Appendix Reference)

In the Appendix, you'll find ready-to-use tools:

- *Forgiveness Reflection Journal Prompts*
- *Sample Scripts for Conflict Resolution Conversations*
- *Prayer Guide for Forgiveness and Workplace Restoration*

(See Appendix A: Workplace Restoration Toolkit for immediate resources.)

Prayer: Lord, Teach Me to Lead with Forgiveness

Father God,

You are the God of mercy, redemption, and new beginnings. Today, I come before You not as a perfect leader or team member, but as a willing one, ready to lay down pride, resentment, and the weight of past wounds so that I may rise in the freedom and strength that only forgiveness brings.

Lord, teach me what it truly means to lead like You. You who forgave freely, restored fully, and saw potential where others saw failure. Help me model that kind of grace in the spaces where I lead, work, and influence.

Forgive me, God, for the grudges I've held in silence. For the harsh words spoken behind closed doors. For the assumptions I've made without seeking understanding. For the hurt I've carried because it felt safer than letting go. I lay it all at Your feet now. I choose to release it, not because they deserve it, but because You've forgiven me for far more.

I declare today that forgiveness is not weakness. It is wisdom, leadership, and Kingdom power in motion.

Heal the places in my heart that still ache from betrayal, criticism, or disappointment. Help me see others through Your eyes, not as problems to fix, but as people to love. Remind me that everyone is fighting battles I can't see. Let empathy soften my tone and humility guide my steps.

Lord, make my workplace a sanctuary of second chances. Let conversations be honest, not harsh. Let correction be covered in compassion. Let conflict lead to connection, not division. And where mistakes have been made, let mercy be the bridge to restoration.

Empower me to lead by example: to apologize when I've been wrong, to forgive when I've been hurt, and to protect the dignity of every person in the room.

Help me create a culture where people can fail forward, speak freely, and grow boldly, because they know forgiveness is the soil we're planting in. May my leadership carry the fragrance of Christ, full of grace and truth, courage and compassion.

I declare:

- *I am a restorer, not a record-keeper.*
- *I am a builder of trust, not a bearer of grudges.*
- *I am a leader who forgives quickly, loves deeply, and moves forward boldly.*

Let forgiveness be the legacy I leave, grace be the culture I create, and restoration be the banner You raise over every team, meeting, and mission I touch.

In Jesus' Name, Amen.

CHAPTER 10

Boundaries that Heal, Not Harden

The Sacred Power of Boundaries

Healthy workplaces begin with healthy people. And healthy people are those who have learned to honor the divine gift of boundaries.

Boundaries aren't barriers that shut others out; *they're gates of wisdom that guard what matters most.* They are a form of sacred stewardship, protecting the treasures God has placed within us: our time, our energy, our emotions, our creativity, and our peace.

But boundaries don't just protect our inner world; they also safeguard the people God has entrusted to us: our families, spouses, children, and friends. When we set boundaries with love and intention, we create space to show up more fully, both at work and at home.

Boundaries that heal are not harsh, they're holy. They are firm, but kind. Strong, but rooted in love. They do not demand control; they invite respect. They protect the heart without punishing others.

When boundaries are communicated clearly, upheld consistently, and modeled by leadership, they create a workplace culture where:

- People are respected, not used.
- Energy is preserved, not drained.
- Communication is clear, not clouded by guilt or

guessing.
- Relationships flourish, rather than collapse under the weight of resentment or exhaustion.

Boundaries give space for excellence without exploitation, productivity without burnout, and community without codependency. They are one of the most powerful ways we live out Proverbs 4:23:

Above all else, guard your heart, for everything you do flows from it. —Proverbs 4:23, NIV

God has entrusted you with a heart, your emotional and spiritual center, and everything in your life flows from it. Boundaries are one of the primary ways you protect what God has placed within you.

They aren't selfish; they're strategic. They're not just personal decisions; they're spiritual life and leadership tools.

Boundaries create the margin needed for healing, clarity, and restoration to take root in your life, your relationships, and the environments where you live, work, and lead.

Why Boundaries Are Essential in the Workplace

Without healthy boundaries, burnout becomes inevitable. Resentment festers in the shadows. Miscommunication breeds unnecessary conflict. Work bleeds endlessly into personal life, damaging our health and our families, communities, ministries, and callings. Talent is squandered, not because it wasn't there, but because *exhaustion replaced inspiration.*

But when compassionate, clear boundaries are in place:

- Teams thrive with newfound focus and collabora-

tion.
- Creativity blossoms as minds and hearts are refreshed.
- Leadership strengthens as trust and respect deepen.
- People grow into their best selves, fueled by grace instead of drained by striving.

Boundaries aren't selfish; they are acts of wisdom, humility, and stewardship. They are love in action for ourselves, others, and the mission we are called to serve.

What Healthy Boundaries Look Like at Work

Healthy boundaries in the workplace are not about control or avoidance; they're about clarity, respect, and sustainability. They create the space for people to bring their best, not burn out trying to give it all.

Here's what healthy boundaries look like in a thriving workplace:

Clear Communication

- Saying "yes" with intention, not obligation.
- Saying "no" without guilt or overexplaining.
- Asking for clarity when expectations are vague or unreasonable.
- Letting others know your availability and capacity with kindness and firmness.

Respect for Time and Energy

- Honoring work hours and personal time without constant interruption.

- Taking breaks and time off without apologizing.
- Avoiding back-to-back meetings with no time to refuel.
- Recognizing when you need to pause, breathe, or reset.

Emotional and Relational Safety

- Refusing to gossip or participate in toxic conversations.
- Protecting your peace by stepping away from unhealthy dynamics.
- Not absorbing the emotions of others or carrying burdens that aren't yours to carry.
- Being honest about your limits without fear of being seen as weak.

Leading by Example

- Modeling rest, sabbath rhythms, and balance as a leader.
- Encouraging your team to prioritize well-being, not just performance.
- Holding space for both accountability and compassion.
- Creating systems that support boundaries (like email-free weekends or mental health check-ins).

How to Build Boundaries That Heal, Not Harden

Here's how you begin building boundaries that don't isolate people, but invite healthier relationships:

1. **Communicate Clearly:** Share your boundaries before

they are crossed. Clear communication prevents future resentment and confusion.

Empowerment Strategy: Use simple, gracious language, such as, "I'm available for calls until 5 PM," or "I'll need 24 hours to review large documents before meetings."

Biblical Wisdom:

> *Let your yes be yes and your no be no.*
> — *Matthew 5:37, NKJV*

2. **Say No (With Respect and Courage):** Saying "no" wisely honors both your capacity and your calling. Every "yes" to something unhealthy is a "no" to something God-given.

Healing Practice: Respond to requests with grace: "Thank you for thinking of me, but I'm at capacity and can't take this on right now."

3. **Follow Through with Your Boundaries:** A boundary is only as powerful as your commitment to uphold it.

Empowerment Strategy: If you've declared that you're unavailable after 6 PM, honor it, lovingly but firmly.

4. **Take Time Off:** Rest is not a luxury; it's a Biblical command and a leadership strategy. (Exodus 20:8-10).

Healing Practice: Schedule regular rest days, and treat them as special, valuable appointments with God for your restoration.

5. Define Your Work Hours: Set a start and end time for your workday, even if you work remotely. Communicate this clearly to your team and family, and consistently honor it.

6. Honor Your Boundaries Without Apology: Protecting your peace protects the quality of what you offer to others. Boundaries are not burdens; they are blessings.

7. Respect Others' Boundaries: Model the respect you wish to receive. Honoring others' boundaries fosters mutual trust and dignity.

Biblical Wisdom:

> *So then, in everything treat others the same way you want them to treat you... — Matthew 7:12, AMP*

8. Set Limits on Tasks and Commitments: Everything good isn't necessarily your assignment. Prayerfully discern what to take on and what to release.

9. Set Technology Boundaries: Technology is an excellent servant but a terrible master. Protect your sacred spaces from constant digital invasion.

Healing Practice: Turn off email notifications after hours. Leave your phone in another room during family time or Sabbath rest.

10. Consider Setting Boundaries Early On: Early boundary setting prevents future awkwardness and resentment.

Empowerment Strategy: During onboarding or project kickoffs, clarify your working hours, response times, and communication preferences.

11. Delegate Wisely: Delegation is not weakness; it's wise stewardship. By delegating, you develop others and protect your own energy for what matters most.

12. Set Priorities According to Purpose: Not everything is urgent. Not everything is yours to carry.

Biblical Wisdom:

> *There is a season (a time appointed) for everything and a time for every delight and event or purpose under heaven.*
> — *Ecclesiastes 3:1, AMP.*

13. Avoid Office Gossip: Gossip is a boundary violation disguised as casual conversation. Redirect gossip with kindness and strength.

Empowerment Strategy: When gossip arises, gently say: "I think it's best if we encourage them directly."

14. Set Emotional Boundaries: You are responsible for your own emotions, and others are responsible for theirs. Don't absorb emotional turmoil that isn't yours to carry.

Healing Practice: Pray daily: *"Lord, I surrender what is not mine to fix, heal, or control."*

15. Seek Help When Needed: Healthy boundaries are a skill, and wise people seek help to strengthen them.

Biblical Wisdom:

Plans fail for lack of counsel, but with many advisers they succeed. — Proverbs 15:22), NIV

Healing Boundaries = Healing Workplaces

When individuals set and honor healing boundaries:

- Stress decreases.
- Clarity increases.
- Communication improves.
- Collaboration strengthens.
- Creativity flourishes.
- Purpose reignites.

Boundaries don't divide, they protect connection. Boundaries don't hinder excellence; they unleash it. Healed hearts create healed boundaries. Healed boundaries create healed workplaces. And healed workplaces create ripples of restoration across families, communities, and nations.

Boundary Reflection Guide: Where Do You Need to Guard Your Heart?

Use the following questions as a journaling prompt or team reflection to begin identifying where God may be inviting you to establish or strengthen boundaries:

1. Where do I feel consistently drained at work, and why?

Is it a certain task, relationship, or expectation? What boundary might restore peace or balance there?

2. Am I saying "yes" to things I know I don't have

the time, energy, or peace to carry?

What is motivating that "yes"? Fear? Guilt? People-pleasing?

3. Do I struggle to say "no" without overexplaining or apologizing?

What would it feel like to trust that my limits are valid and worth honoring?

4. Have I built space into my week for rest, reflection, or sabbath rhythms?

If not, what's one minor adjustment I can make to honor the life and flow God designed for me?

5. Where do I need to communicate more clearly to protect my peace and purpose?

How can I begin that conversation with kindness and confidence?

Let what you say be simply 'Yes' or 'No'; anything more than this comes from evil. —Matthew 5:37, ESV

Final Encouragement:

Boundaries are not about pushing people away, they're about protecting what God has placed within you. When you lead from a place of wholeness, others are invited to do the same.

And as more people step into healing, peace, and clarity, your workplace becomes a sanctuary of restoration, not just a center of productivity.

Reflection Questions

1. Where in my work life am I currently violating my own boundaries out of fear, guilt, or habit?
2. What new boundary would honor God, my calling, and my relationships?
3. How can I lovingly model better boundaries to my team or coworkers this week?

Workplace Healing Action Steps

- Write a simple personal *"Boundary Statement"* this week (e.g., "I do not check work emails after 6 PM.").
- Practice saying "no" graciously one time this week when a boundary is challenged.
- Identify one small technology boundary you can implement to create more sacred space and time for rest and renewal.

Destiny Declarations

Speak these aloud boldly in faith:

- *Through Christ, I steward my time, energy, and calling with wisdom and joy.*
- *My boundaries are gates of grace, not walls of fear.*
- *I honor God, myself, and others by living and leading with healthy, healing boundaries.*

Workplace Restoration Toolkit (Appendix Reference)

Inside Appendix A, you'll find:

- *Boundary Setting Worksheet for Professionals*
- *Sample Scripts for Respectful Boundary Conversations*
- *Technology Detox Guide for Work-Life Balance*

(See the complete Toolkit for practical exercises you can implement immediately.)

Prayer: Lord, Help Me Set Boundaries That Heal

Heavenly Father,

You are the God of order, peace, and purpose. I thank You that You are not a God of confusion, chaos, or burnout. You lovingly call me to a life that is *full* but not frantic, *fruitful* but not frantic. So today, I surrender the pressure, the guilt, and the striving, and I ask You to teach me how to set boundaries that heal, not harden.

Lord, show me where I said *"yes"* when You called me to say *"no."* Reveal the places where fear, people-pleasing, or insecurity have caused me to overextend, overcommit, or overlook my own well-being. I repent for every moment I traded Your peace for performance. Today, I choose to live by grace, not grind.

Help me see boundaries not as barriers, but as blessings. Give me the courage to say "no" with kindness and conviction and the humility to honor my limits without apology. Teach me to communicate clearly, lead wisely, and protect the gifts You've entrusted to me: my time, my energy, my peace, and my purpose.

God, let my boundaries reflect Your heart, not cold or cutting, but compassionate and clear. Let every boundary I set be rooted in love: love for You, others, and the mission

You've given me. May the people around me feel respected, trusted, and whole because I've chosen to lead with integrity and self-stewardship.

Where there's been burnout, restore balance. Where there's been resentment, restore rest. Where there's been silence, teach me to speak in truth and grace. And where I've intentionally or unknowingly violated the boundaries of others, convict me quickly, and lead me gently into reconciliation.

Father, I commit to protecting what matters. I will guard my heart, for everything I do flows from it. Let my boundaries be gates of grace; open enough for love, but firm enough for wisdom.

I declare:

- I am not available for chaos. I am assigned to peace.
- I am not bound by guilt. I am guided by grace.
- I am not called to everything. I am called to what matters most.

Let my life be a model of healthy rhythm, divine order, and sacred boundaries. Let every boundary I set plant a seed of healing at home, work, and in every life I touch.

In the mighty Name of Jesus, Amen.

PART IV:
RESTORING RELATIONSHIPS,
REBUILDING TEAMS

CHAPTER 11

Repairing Broken Bridges at Work

Rebuilding Broken Bridges at Work

Workplace relationships are more than professional connections; they are meaningful bridges. Built over time with trust, shared purpose, and consistent collaboration, these bridges allow something beautiful to flow: communication, creativity, and connection.

But just like physical bridges, relational ones can be damaged, sometimes in an instant. Maybe it was betrayal. A broken promise. A moment of miscommunication that spiraled into silence. Or a leadership misstep that created distance instead of trust.

Whatever the cause, you can feel it when a bridge breaks. Suddenly, everything feels harder. Communication slows. Tension rises. Purpose gets delayed. And the emotional weight of the damage starts to affect not just productivity, but people.

Some walk around these broken bridges daily, pretending the collapse didn't happen. Others quietly build walls to protect themselves from further pain. But either way, something is lost, and everyone feels it.

Here's the good news: Broken bridges can be rebuilt. Trust can be restored. And relationships can come back stronger than before, if we're willing to do the heart work.

But restoration doesn't happen by accident. It takes courage to admit the damage. It takes humility to go first.

It takes wisdom to choose the right time, tone, and approach. And it takes love, real, active, redemptive love, to keep showing up when it would be easier to shut down.

Scripture gives us this clear, compassionate challenge:

If it is possible, as far as it depends on you, live at peace with everyone. —Romans 12:18, AMP

This doesn't mean tolerating abuse or pretending nothing happened. It means asking the Spirit, What depends on me? What can I say? What can I own? What can I release?

In this next section, we'll walk together, step by step, through the process of rebuilding broken bridges at work. Because when healing flows freely again, so does clarity. So does purpose. So does destiny.

Do everything possible on your part to live in peace with everybody. —Romans 12:18, GNT

Steps to Rebuild and Repair Workplace Relationships

Restoring broken relationships at work isn't easy, but it is possible. The process requires emotional maturity, spiritual wisdom, and a profound commitment to healing rather than hiding. Whether you're a leader, team member, or someone quietly hurting behind the scenes, here's a path forward:

Step 1: Reflect Before You Reach Out

Before initiating any conversation, take time to examine your heart.

1. What exactly happened?

2. How did it affect you, and possibly others?
3. Are you seeking restoration, or are you still trying to be "right"?

Ask God to help you see the situation clearly, with compassion and humility.

Search me {thoroughly}, O God, and know my heart; Test me and know my anxious thoughts; —Psalm 139:23, AMP

Step 2: Own Your Part, Even If It's Small

Healthy restoration starts with personal responsibility. You may not be responsible for the entire fracture, but what part can you be held accountable for? Apologize sincerely for anything you contributed, without defending or deflecting.

You hypocrite (play-actor, pretender), first get the log out of your own eye, and then you will see clearly to take the speck out of your brother's eye. —Matthew 7:5, AMP

Step 3: Extend Grace, Before It's Deserved

Rebuilding trust often requires forgiveness before the other person apologizes or makes amends. It's not about excusing the hurt; it's about releasing its power over you.

Be kind and helpful to one another, tender-hearted {compassionate, understanding}, forgiving one another {readily and freely}, just as God in Christ also forgave you. —Ephesians 4:32, AMP

Step 4: Initiate a Conversation With Humility and Clarity

When the time is right, reach out calmly and kindly. Focus on how the situation affected the relationship, not just how it made you feel. Use *"I" statements* and aim for mutual understanding, not blame.

A soft and gentle and thoughtful answer turns away wrath, But harsh and painful and careless words stir up anger.
—Proverbs 15:1, AMP

Step 5: Rebuild Trust Over Time

Don't rush restoration. Trust is earned in consistency, not in one conversation. Be patient with the process, with the person, and with yourself. Celebrate small steps and stay committed to moving forward, even if it's slow progress.

Love bears all things {regardless of what comes}, believes all things {looking for the best in each one}, hopes all things {remaining steadfast during difficult times}, endures all things {without weakening}. —1 Corinthians 13:7, AMP

Guided Reconciliation Exercise: A Personal Walk Toward Peace

Use this exercise for journaling, prayer, or personal reflection *before entering a conversation.* You can also adapt it as a small group or leadership team discussion tool.

1. Identify the Break

- What happened that caused the rupture in this relationship?
- Be specific, but not self-righteous.
- Write down the facts and feelings.

2. Name the Impact

- How has this affected your communication, your trust, your work, or your peace of mind?
- What emotions are still lingering? (anger, grief, disappointment, fear, shame?)

3. Acknowledge Your Part

- What could I have done differently?
- What, if anything, do I need to apologize for?
- Even if your part was small, take full ownership of it.

4. Invite God Into the Pain

- Lord, what do You see in this situation that I don't?
- What do You want to heal in me?
- In them?
- Sit in silence and ask the Holy Spirit to speak to your heart.

5. Release the Offense

I choose to forgive [Name] for [What happened]. I release them and entrust this situation to You, Lord. Say it aloud or write it in your journal as an act of spiritual release.

6. Plan the First Step Toward Peace

What can I do today to take one step toward rebuilding this relationship? Whether it's sending a message, setting a meeting, or simply praying with compassion, choose to act in love.

Prayer: Father, give me the humility to see clearly, the courage to reach out, and the grace to forgive freely. Help me rebuild what's been broken, not in my own strength but in Yours. Where trust has been lost, plant seeds of restoration. Where wounds remain, pour out Your healing. Let Your peace reign in every relationship I touch, so that my workplace becomes a place where You dwell.

In Jesus' Name, Amen.

Practical Steps to Restoration

Step 1: Proactive Communication, The Lifeline of Restoration

Healing begins when we choose courage over silence. Avoiding broken relationships doesn't protect us; it only allows bitterness and misunderstanding to take deeper root.

Empowerment Strategy: Initiate the conversation with humility and hope. You don't have to wait for a perfect moment; you can create one by stepping forward in faith.

Practical Example: Start with these words: *"I value our relationship and would love to repair any damage between us if you're willing to have a conversation."* A single act of brave communication can change everything.

Step 2: Seek Understanding Before Offering Solutions

Healing doesn't begin by defending your perspective. It begins by seeking to understand the other person's heart. True restoration requires us to listen deeply, not just to words but to the emotions and stories behind them.

Biblical Wisdom:

Everyone should be quick to listen, slow to speak, and slow to become angry. —James 1:19, NIV.

Understand this, my beloved brothers and sisters. Let everyone be quick to hear {be a careful, thoughtful listener}, slow to speak {a speaker of carefully chosen words and}, slow to anger {patient, reflective, forgiving}; —James 1:19, AMP

Empowerment Strategy:

Ask heartfelt questions like:

- "Help me understand how you experienced this situation."
- "What hurt you the most about what happened?"

Let understanding become the bridge that reconnects broken hearts.

Step 3: Apologize Sincerely, Even If You Didn't Cause It All

An apology isn't about taking the blame for everything. It's about taking responsibility for your piece of the bridge that fell. Sincere apologies carry healing power because they say: *"I see your pain, and it matters to me."*

Healing Language:

- *"I'm truly sorry for how my actions (or inaction) made you feel."*

- *"I now see how my words impacted you, and I grieve that."*

Step 4: Own the Failure, Together

Even if the brokenness wasn't entirely your fault, owning the reality of what happened shows emotional maturity and leadership. It says, *"We are better than this, and together, we can do better."*

Empowerment Strategy: Speak life into the situation by saying: *"We didn't handle this the best way, and I want to be part of making it right."*

Step 5: Outline the Correction

Forgiveness without change is incomplete. Healing requires tangible action steps.

Practical Tip: Work together to define how things will change:

- Clearer communication?
- New ground rules?
- Regular check-ins to maintain connection?

Restoration becomes real when both hearts commit to a new, healthier way forward.

Step 6: Ask for Help, Effectively and Humbly

Healthy leaders are humble leaders. Healing broken bridges often means asking: *"What do you need from me to feel safe, supported, and valued going forward?"* This simple question empowers others to own their role in the restoration journey.

Step 7: Evaluate Team Performance, Together

Reflection is vital to lasting restoration. Create safe, honest spaces to evaluate what's working, what's not, and how to keep growing as a team, without blame or shame.

Step 8: Rebuild Trust Day by Day

Trust is rebuilt slowly, not in one grand moment but through daily acts of consistency, honesty, and kindness.

Biblical Wisdom:

Whoever walks in integrity walks securely, but whoever takes crooked paths will be found out. — Proverbs 10:9, NIV.

Healing Practice: Show up, follow through, and keep your word, even in small things. Trust is restored drop by drop.

Step 9: Celebrate Small Wins and Successes

Healing journeys can feel long, but celebrating small wins keeps hope alive.

Empowerment Strategy: Publicly acknowledge moments of honesty, bravery, collaboration, and kindness. Recognize every step of restoration, no matter how small.

Step 10: Set New Team Goals Together

New goals create new momentum. Use collaborative goal-setting to reunite your team around shared purpose and vision.

Practical Tip: Include relational goals too:

- We will hold monthly check-ins to build connection.
- We will encourage at least one person per week.

Step 11: Acknowledge the Breakdown and Address It Openly

Pretending nothing happened only deepens wounds. Acknowledging pain, gently, courageously, and prayerfully, paves the way for authentic healing.

Step 12: Manage Expectations Wisely

Healing is a journey, not a sprint. Set realistic expectations for progress and celebrate growth, even when it's slow and imperfect.

Step 13: Provide Strong, Compassionate Leadership

Restoring broken bridges requires leadership rooted in grace, accountability, and unwavering hope.

Biblical Wisdom:

> *The greatest one among you must be your servant.*
> — *Matthew 23:11, GNT*

When leaders lead with love, restoration becomes the natural culture.

Step 14: Foster a Healing Team Culture

Create a team environment that breathes life, trust, and renewal through simple practices like:

Team Games and Bonding Activities:

Build trust through shared positive experiences.

1. *Acknowledging Broken Trust:* Speak truth, not denial.
2. *Believing in Your Team:* Speak life daily.
3. *Coaching for Well-Being:* Support mental, emotional, physical, and spiritual health.
4. *Creating an Inclusive Culture:* Honor every voice and background.
5. *Encouraging Cooperation:* Celebrate shared wins, not individual egos.
6. *Focusing on Team Cohesion:* Make unity a daily focus.
7. *Leveraging Shared Daily Journaling:* Reflect on wins, gratitude, and lessons together.
8. *Motivating Through Vision:* Paint a compelling picture of the future you're building together.

Biblical Model of Restoration

God is the ultimate bridge-builder:

- He initiates reconciliation (Romans 5:8)
- He forgives fully (Isaiah 43:25)
- He restores completely (Joel 2:25)

When we model His heart at work, we don't just re-build teams, we usher in His wisdom and His Kingdom in boardrooms, breakrooms, and Zoom calls.

Reflection Questions

1. Where have I allowed broken relationships at work to go unaddressed?
2. What part can I humbly own, even if I wasn't entirely at fault?
3. What one courageous step toward reconciliation can I take today?

Workplace Healing Action Step

- Reach out to one coworker or teammate with whom trust needs to be rebuilt. Initiate a healing conversation.
- Lead a team reflection session focused on gratitude, lessons learned, and relationship goals.
- Create a simple *"Trust Pact"* with your team; a few commitments to guide your communication, forgiveness, and restoration culture.

Destiny Declaration

Speak these aloud over your heart, your team, and your workplace:

- *Through Christ, I am a builder of bridges, not walls.*
- *I bring healing conversations and courageous leadership wherever I go.*
- *No division is too great for God's restoration power working through me.*

Workplace Restoration Toolkit (Appendix Reference)

In the Appendix, you'll find:

- *Healing Conversation Templates*
- *Team Trust Rebuilding Worksheet*
- *Shared Team Journaling Prompts for Restoration*

(See Appendix A for easy-to-use tools to start restoring today.)

Prayer: Lord, Make Me a Bridge-Builder

Heavenly Father,

You are the God who restores, rebuilds, and never leaves broken things in pieces. I thank You that nothing is too fractured for Your healing hand: no relationship is too far gone, no mistake is too great, and no silence is too long. You are the Master Bridge-Builder, and today, I invite You to work through me.

Lord, I confess that I've allowed some bridges to break. Whether through hurt, pride, fear, or avoidance, I've stepped back when You may have been calling me to step forward. I ask for Your forgiveness, and I receive Your grace. Give me the courage to face what's been fractured; not to control the outcome, but to walk in obedience, humility, and love.

Help me see people through Your eyes, not as opponents but as image-bearers, not as problems but as purpose-filled souls. Teach me how to listen without defending, to speak with tenderness, not tension, and to lead with compassion, not control.

I ask You now, God, heal the workplace bridges I've been a part of breaking. Restore the trust, rebuild the unity, and renew the respect. Show me where to begin: who to call, what to say, when to be silent, and when to speak boldly. Let me be known not for holding grudges, but for holding space where grace can flow.

And when I grow weary in the waiting, remind me that restoration is not my burden to carry alone; it's a journey we walk together, with You at the center. The battles I face belong to You (2 Chronicles 20:15, 2 Chronicles 20:17). I lay them on Your altar in prayer, and trust that You are with me on this journey.

Please make me consistent in my integrity, generous in my forgiveness, and wise in my responses. Let my life testify that healing is always possible and that love always makes a way.

I declare:

- *I am not called to build walls; I am called to build bridges.*
- *I am not bound by bitterness; I am filled with grace.*
- *I am not afraid of restoration; I am an agent of it.*

Lord, breathe on every broken relationship, every tense team dynamic, every silent space between coworkers, and begin healing today. Let Your presence transform the culture of my workplace, one bridge at a time.

In Jesus' Name, Amen

CHAPTER 12

Leadership Reimagined:
Love, Courage, and Integrity

A New Kind of Leader

The world is not desperate for louder voices, stronger personalities, sharper suits, or more polished performances. What it desperately needs is something far more profound, a new kind of leader.

A leader whose strength flows not from ego or title, but from heart, spirit, and character. One who leads not to be seen, but to serve. One who chooses love over fear, courage over comfort, and integrity over image, even when it costs them something.

We are crying out for leaders who are not just chasing profits, but building people. Leaders who don't see their teams as tools, but as souls. Leaders who are not merely bosses, but Restorers. Restorers of trust. Restorers of peace. Restorers of purpose.

Jesus redefined greatness when He said, "Whoever wants to be great among you must be your servant." (Matthew 20:26). In a culture that celebrates climbing ladders, Kingdom leadership looks more like washing feet.

In this chapter, we will reimagine leadership through the lens of God's design. A leadership model built on love, courage, and integrity. These aren't just admirable traits for a mission statement. They are essential foundations for workplaces that foster healing, growth, and lasting change. The kind of change that reaches beyond boardrooms and bottom lines into families, communities, and generations. This is leadership that restores.

Why Leadership Must Be Reimagined

The traditional leadership model, characterized by a top-down approach, fear-based tactics, and a focus on control, is collapsing. And truthfully, it needs to.

Because the next generation isn't impressed by titles. They're not drawn to corner offices or authoritarian commands. They're not willing to sacrifice their well-being for shallow authority or empty promises of success.

They're looking for something deeper, something real. They want purpose over position. Authenticity over intimidation. Collaboration over control. And inspiration over fear. And they're not afraid to walk away from environments that refuse to evolve.

Organizations that cling to outdated leadership mindsets, ones that value results over relationships, compliance over compassion, will watch their brightest, most innovative people leave. Not because they're unwilling to work hard, but because they refuse to work wounded.

They're searching for places where their hearts, not just their hands, are valued. Where they're treated like people, not parts in a machine. Where leadership doesn't demand performance, it draws out purpose.

If we're truly serious about restoring workplaces, we must take leadership reimagining seriously.

Leadership must be viewed not as a crown to wear, but as a cross to carry because Kingdom leadership doesn't seek status. It seeks to steward. It doesn't lord over people; it lifts them up. It doesn't compete for power; it creates space for others to rise.

Authentic leadership is about recognizing the sacred responsibility of those around you:

- To see the gifts in them.
- To protect their destiny.
- To call out what's broken,
- And to build what's missing with courage, humility, and love.

The world doesn't need another self-made empire. It needs leaders who restore those who are willing to lead like Jesus: not by climbing to the top, but by kneeling low, carrying the cross of servanthood, and lifting others into their God-given purpose.

The Core Principles of Restorative Leadership

True leadership, the kind that heals workplaces and unlocks destinies, is built on *three unshakable pillars:*

Love, Courage, and Integrity.

Let's take a closer look at each one:

1. Leading with Love: Building Trust and Belonging

Leading with love means using empathy, compassion, and care as your primary leadership language. It means seeing people not as cogs in a corporate machine, but as souls entrusted to your stewardship.

Leading with love looks like:

- Listening deeply to your employees' struggles,

hopes, and dreams.

- Recognizing people for who they are, not just what they produce.
- Creating cultures of psychological safety where every voice matters.
- Extending grace when mistakes happen instead of wielding shame.
- Encouraging wholeness over hustle.

Practical Actions:

1. Begin meetings with personal check-ins: "How are you, really?"
2. Celebrate life milestones: birthdays, graduations, family wins, not just project deadlines.
3. Offer regular encouragement, without waiting for an annual review.

Biblical Wisdom:

Beyond all these things put on and wrap yourselves in {unselfish} love, which is the perfect bond of unity {for everything is bound together in agreement when each one seeks the best for others}.
— *Colossians 3:14, AMP*

Love binds teams together far more powerfully than policies or procedures ever could.

2. Leading with Courage: Speaking Truth and Taking Risks

Leading with courage means choosing boldness over fear, even when it costs you something. Courageous leadership looks like:

- Speaking up for what's right, even when it's unpopular.
- Advocating for the overlooked, the unheard, and the marginalized.
- Admitting when you don't have all the answers.
- Taking calculated risks to innovate, even when it feels safer to maintain the status quo.
- Empowering others to lead, not hoarding control for yourself.

Practical Actions:

1. Publicly support ethical decisions, even if they are inconvenient.
2. Encourage healthy disagreement during brainstorming; innovation thrives in diversity of thought.
3. Ask your team regularly: "What risks should we be brave enough to take this quarter?"

Biblical Wisdom:

Be strong and courageous. Do not be afraid; do not be discouraged, for the Lord your God will be with you wherever you go.
—Joshua 1:9, NIV.

True courage is not fearlessness. It is faithfulness despite fear. It is remembering that God is with you wherever you go.

3. Leading with Integrity: Modeling Excellence and Accountability

Integrity is the invisible armor of authentic leadership. It's living so that your life matches your leadership, both in private and in public.

Integrity looks like:

- Keeping your word even when it's inconvenient.
- Admitting mistakes and making things right.
- Refusing to participate in gossip, favoritism, or double standards.
- Protecting the dignity of every person in your sphere of influence.
- Modeling the behaviors you expect from others without exception.

Practical Actions:

1. Follow through on every promise, no matter how small.
2. Be transparent about decision-making.
3. Create clear and fair policies that are just and consistently applied.

Biblical Wisdom:

The righteous man who walks in integrity and lives life in accord with his {godly} beliefs—How blessed {happy and spiritually secure} are his children after him {who have his example to follow}.
— *Proverbs 20:7, AMP*

When leaders walk in integrity, they leave a legacy that blesses generations.

Practical Problem-Solving for Modern Leadership Challenges

Restorative leadership is not just a philosophy; it is a daily practice. Here are a few transformational strategies to make it real:

1. Empower Employees:

- Equip and unleash others to lead, not just follow.
- Delegate meaningful tasks, not just busywork.
- Involve employees in setting goals and solving problems.
- Create leadership development opportunities at every level.

2. Foster Emotional Intelligence: Great leaders know how to manage their emotions and how to honor the emotions of others.

- Offer emotional intelligence training.
- Normalize empathy, compassion, and reflection.
- Prioritize Continuous Learning: the best leaders are constantly becoming better.
- Celebrate learning, not just outcomes.
- Fund leadership development programs and mentorships.
- Host "learning lunches" to discuss new ideas, books, or podcasts

3. Model Transparency and Trust:

- Don't ask for what you're unwilling to live yourself.
- Share both successes and failures.
- Celebrate vulnerability as a leadership strength.

How to Lead with Love, Courage, and Integrity Day-to-Day

- *Create Psychological Safety:* Show that questions and concerns are welcome.
- *Communicate Openly:* Be honest about challenges and invite collaboration.
- *Be Authentic:* Lead with realness, not performance.
- *Set Ethical Standards:* Lead by example.
- *Practice Gratitude:* Regularly thank people for who they are, not just what they do.
- *Speak Life:* Let your words heal, empower, and elevate.

Death and life are in the power of the tongue, and those who love it and indulge it will eat its fruit and bear the consequences of their words. —Proverbs 18:21, AMP

As leaders, we must choose life daily.

Biblical Models of Restorative Leadership

The Bible isn't just a record of history; it's a living blueprint for how to lead with wisdom, humility, and power under God's authority. Throughout Scripture, we encounter leaders who did far more than build systems or win battles. They restored people.

They weren't driven by ego or status, but by vision, sacrifice, and love. These were leaders who understood that influence is a stewardship, not a spotlight. They carried burdens that weren't theirs to prove their greatness, but to release others into theirs.

In a world where leadership is too often defined by dominance, competition, or charisma, these men and women remind us of a higher way, *a Kingdom way.*

They walked in alignment with God's heart. They led with compassion in times of chaos. They chose obedience over popularity, and service over self. And their stories aren't just inspirational, they're deeply practical.

They offer timeless blueprints for what leadership can and should look like in today's workplaces. Leadership that heals. Leadership that builds. Leadership that lasts.

Let's take a closer look at three extraordinary leaders who modeled the essence of restorative leadership, and what their examples reveal about how we are called to lead today.

1. Jesus: The Servant Leader Who Healed Through Humility

Key Passage: John 13:12–17

When Jesus, King of Kings, the very Son of God, knelt to wash the dust-covered feet of His disciples, He wasn't simply performing an act of kindness. He was redefining leadership forever.

In a culture where power was measured by position and greatness was marked by control, Jesus introduced a radical shift:

- He led with a towel, not a title.
- He healed through presence, not performance.
- He restored with love, not leverage.

This wasn't just humility, it was holy authority cloaked in compassion.

Jesus showed that real leadership doesn't intimidate or demand: it invites, it lowers itself, and it lifts others up.

In that one sacred moment in the upper room, Jesus silenced the world's definition of success and whispered Heaven's definition of greatness.

He didn't posture for influence; He poured Himself out for it. He didn't seek applause; He sought alignment with the Father. And in doing so, He gave us a gold standard for every leader who longs to build more than numbers, who longs to restore people.

In workplaces marked by ego battles, burnout, and broken trust, Jesus' way of leadership still brings healing, not through domination, but through devotion, not through climbing over others, but by bending down in love.

Now that I, your Lord and Teacher, have washed your feet, you also should wash one another's feet. —John 13:14, NIV

Restorative Leadership Lesson: You don't need to be the loudest voice in the room. You need to be the one willing to serve first, love most, and stay when others walk away. That's what Jesus did. And that's the kind of leadership that still turns the world upside down.

2. Nehemiah: The Rebuilder Who Led with Vision and Grit

Key Passage: Nehemiah 2:17–18

Nehemiah wasn't a priest. He wasn't a prophet. He was a cupbearer, a civic and marketplace leader whose job was to serve in the palace, not the temple.

And yet, when he heard that the walls of Jerusalem were in ruins, he didn't say, *"That's not my place."* He allowed the burden to break his heart, and then he let that brokenness birth a vision.

Nehemiah didn't just grieve over what was lost. He got to work. He prayed with intensity. He planned with wisdom. And he partnered with others, rallying ordinary people to do something extraordinary.

What sets Nehemiah apart is not that he avoided opposition; it's that he stayed anchored in purpose when the opposition came. He didn't let criticism stop him. He didn't let fatigue derail him. He didn't let fear silence him.

He saw rubble, and chose to see blueprints instead. He stepped into the mess with strategy, grit, and spiritual conviction. And in doing so, he didn't just rebuild walls, he restored identity, unity, and purpose to a fractured people.

Nehemiah is proof that leadership doesn't require a pulpit to be anointed. It requires a willing heart, a God-given vision, and the courage to say: **Let us rise up and build.**

And I told them of the hand of my God which had been good upon me, and also of the king's words that he had spoken to me. So they said, "Let us rise up and build." Then they set their hands to this good work. —Nehemiah 2:18, NKJV

Restorative Leadership Lesson: Healing begins with someone who sees brokenness and says, "We don't have to stay here." You don't need a perfect plan; you need a faithful yes. Your workplace might feel like rubble right now: damaged trust, low morale, scattered vision.

But with God, your burden can become a blueprint, and your leadership can become the spark that starts rebuilding what's been broken.

3. Deborah: The Wise Warrior Who Led with Boldness and Discernment

Key Passage: Judges 4:4–10

Deborah was a prophet, a judge, and a military leader, a combination almost unheard of in her day, *and still rare in ours.*

Yet she didn't wait for cultural permission or widespread consensus to lead. She rose from a place of quiet strength, spiritual clarity, and unwavering trust in God.

Deborah didn't lead from insecurity or comparison. She led from overflow, the overflow of God's wisdom, presence, and peace. She listened carefully. She discerned wisely. And when the moment came to act, she moved with bold, Spirit-led courage.

When others hesitated, she said, "I will go." Not out of pride, but out of purpose. She stood firm when the nation was unsure. She spoke when others were silent. She partnered with others, but she never outsourced her obedience to God.

Deborah's leadership reminds us that restorative leadership requires both courage and clarity. It's not loud or showy; it's faithful and firm. It's the kind of leadership that rises to meet the moment, not for applause, but for Kingdom impact.

She shows us that boldness and humility are not opposites; they are powerful partners in the hands of a wise leader.

And she said, "I will surely go with you. Nevertheless, the road on which you are going will not lead to your glory, for the Lord will sell Sisera into the hand of a woman." Then Deborah arose and went with Barak to Kedesh. —Judges 4:9, ESV

Restorative Leadership Lesson: You don't need permission to rise when God has already anointed you. You don't have to lead like anyone else, just lead like the Spirit-filled, called leader God made you to be. Lead with wisdom. Lead with boldness. Lead with faith.

The Deborahs of today are not waiting; they're already standing. And the world is desperate for their voice.

4. Joseph: The Forgiving Leader Who Turned Pain Into Purpose

Key Passage: Genesis 50:20

Joseph's story is marked by betrayal, injustice, and loss. Rejected by his brothers, sold into slavery, falsely accused, and forgotten in prison. Joseph experienced more workplace trauma than most of us could imagine.

And yet, through every injustice, Joseph remained faithful. He didn't allow bitterness to take root. He didn't let hardship harden his heart. By the time Joseph rose to power in Egypt, second only to Pharaoh, he wasn't driven by revenge.

He was moved by purpose. When the very brothers who betrayed him came seeking help during a famine, Joseph had every right to retaliate. Instead, he forgave them. He chose restoration over revenge. Purpose over pain.

You intended to harm me, but God intended it for good to accomplish what is now being done, the saving of many lives.
—Genesis 50:20, NIV

Joseph didn't just forgive; he redeemed the pain by aligning it with God's greater plan. His leadership didn't erase what happened; it transformed it into something redemptive.

Restorative Leadership Lesson: Pain doesn't disqualify you from leadership; it prepares you for it. True leaders don't just rise despite their wounds; they rise because they've let God heal them. Forgiveness is what frees your influence and multiplies your impact.

5. Moses: The Reluctant Leader Who Found Strength in God's Presence

Key Passage: Exodus 3:10–12

Moses didn't ask to be a leader. In fact, when God called him to lead, he resisted: *"Who am I that I should go?"* He felt unqualified, unworthy, and unprepared. And yet, God wasn't looking for perfection; He was looking for willingness.

Despite his fears, his failures, and his past, Moses stepped into leadership. And he led not by leaning on charisma or credentials, but by returning again and again to the presence of God. Moses didn't move without God's direction. He didn't speak without God's guidance.

He led an entire nation out of slavery not because he was fearless, but because he was faithful. His leadership reminds us that God doesn't just call the ready; He equips the called. The most powerful leadership tool Moses had wasn't his staff; it was his intimacy with God.

The Lord replied, "My Presence will go with you, and I will give you rest." —Exodus 33:14, NIV

Restorative Leadership Lesson: You don't have to feel ready to be used. Restorative leaders don't rely on their own strength; they rely on the presence of God. If God called you to it, He will meet you in it.

6. Barnabas: The Encourager Who Elevated Others into Destiny

Key Passage: Acts 9:26–28

Barnabas is often known as "the son of encouragement," and for good reason. While others doubted Paul's transformation, Barnabas saw his potential.

When others turned away, Barnabas leaned in. He used his credibility to advocate for someone others feared. He saw not just who Paul had been, but who he was becoming.

Barnabas wasn't the loudest leader. He wasn't driven by ego or platform. He led by lifting others. He gave second chances. He made space at the table.

Later, when John Mark failed on a missionary journey, it was Barnabas who gave him another opportunity, an act that helped restore John Mark's calling and eventually led to his authorship of the Gospel that bears his name.

Barnabas reminds us that encouragement isn't fluff; it's fuel. And believing in someone before they believe in themselves is one of the most powerful forms of leadership there is.

Restorative Leadership Lesson: Your encouragement can unlock someone else's calling. Restorative leaders elevate others. They speak life into what's dormant. They don't compete; they cultivate. And in doing so, they expand the Kingdom beyond what they could build alone.

Your Invitation to Walk in Their Footsteps

Restorative leadership isn't reserved for the pulpit or the spotlight. It's not defined by charisma, title, or tenure. It's a sacred posture of the heart, a daily willingness to see what's broken and say, *"Here I am, Lord. Use me."*

Throughout Scripture, we're given living proof that God can work through any vessel willing to be poured out in love, courage, and humility:

1. **Jesus, the Servant King**, who knelt to wash feet and led with presence instead of pride. He reminds us that leadership begins with service, and healing begins with love.
2. **Nehemiah, the visionary builder**, who didn't wait for permission to care. He saw ruins and responded with prayer, strategy, and grit. He turned rubble into revival.
3. **Deborah, the wise warrior**, who rose in boldness and discernment when others hesitated. She led not with noise, but with conviction and clarity birthed in God's presence.
4. **Joseph, the forgiving leader**, who turned betrayal into blessing. He chose mercy over revenge and allowed purpose to rise from pain.
5. **Moses, the reluctant shepherd,** who led not because he was fearless, but because he stayed close to God's presence. His strength came not from his confidence, but from his communion.
6. **Barnabas, the quiet encourager**, who lifted others into their destinies. He saw potential in the overlooked and offered second chances that changed the course of history.

None of these leaders were perfect. But each of them made a choice, to align with Heaven's perspective, to carry hope where there was brokenness, and to lead with a heart that made space for restoration.

And now, it's your turn. Whether you lead a team, a

household, a classroom, a company, an organization, a congregation, or simply the atmosphere around your desk...

You are invited into the same holy work: To lead with humility like Jesus. To build with vision like Nehemiah. To rise in courage like Deborah. To forgive like Joseph. To trust like Moses. To encourage like Barnabas.

This isn't just about workplace culture. It's about *eternal impact*. Because the workplace is more than a job; it's a mission field. A platform where lives are shaped, dignity is restored, and God's presence can transform not just what we do, but who we become.

The call to restorative leadership is not about doing more. It's about becoming more, more compassionate, more Spirit-led, and more like Christ. And it starts not with a strategy, but with a surrendered heart.

This is your invitation. Not to climb higher, but to go deeper. Not to perform harder, but to love better. Not to wait for someone else to fix it, but to rise and rebuild.

The world doesn't need more noise. It needs more Nehemiahs. More Deborahs. More Josephs. More Jesus-followers willing to lead with heaven in mind.

The workplace is ready. The harvest is great. And the Restorer is calling. ***Will you walk in their footsteps?***

Reflection Questions

1. Which leadership style (love, courage, or integrity) do I naturally embody?
2. Which one do I need to strengthen right now?
3. What is one small leadership habit I could start today to lead more like Jesus?

Workplace Healing Action Steps

This week, choose one leadership behavior, love, courage, or integrity, to model intentionally. Host a team conversation: *"What does great leadership look like to you?"* Take one courageous step you've been postponing, and do it prayerfully.

Destiny Declarations

Speak these aloud with boldness and faith:

- *Through Christ, I lead with love, courage, and unwavering integrity.*
- *I empower others by lifting them higher, not standing over them.*
- *I create workplaces where hearts heal, teams thrive, and destinies are fulfilled.*

Workplace Restoration Toolkit (Appendix Reference)
In the Appendix, you'll find:

- *Leadership Self-Reflection Inventory*
- *Sample Team Discussion Guide: Reimagining Leadership*
- *Courageous Conversations Framework for Leaders*

(See Appendix A for tools you can use today to transform your leadership culture.)

Prayer: Lord, Shape Me into a Restorative Leader

Gracious Father,

You are the ultimate Leader, full of wisdom, power, love, and truth. I thank You for calling me not just to positions, titles, or tasks, but to the holy work of leadership that heals. I surrender my ego, my striving, my fears, and my old models of control. Shape me now into the kind of leader this world so desperately needs, one formed in Your image, led by Your Spirit, and anchored in Your Word.

Lord, teach me to lead with love, see people the way You see them, listen with compassion, and speak life where discouragement has taken root. Let my leadership create belonging, not burnout, and connection, not control.

Teach me to lead with courage; to do what's right even when it's risky, to advocate for those who are unseen, to admit when I fall short, and to rise with resilience and humility. May my boldness be birthed in prayer, not pride.

And above all, Lord, teach me to lead with integrity, to align my private life with my public message, to honor every commitment, to be trustworthy in the small things, and to lead by example without compromise.

Father, I invite You to reimagine my leadership. Strip away anything that hinders, distracts, or divides. Replace it with clarity, character, and conviction. Make my leadership a mirror of Christ: a leadership that washes feet, rebuilds walls, and stands strong in wisdom and grace.

I declare:

- *I am a leader who loves deeply, lives courageously, and leads with unwavering integrity.*
- *I do not lead for applause; I lead for impact.*
- *I am not building my own empire; I'm stewarding a Kingdom assignment.*

Let my life be a living testimony that servant leadership still changes lives and that one surrendered heart can transform an entire workplace culture. Anoint me now, God, for this sacred task: to manage, multiply, mend, and mobilize.

Let Your Kingdom come through every meeting, every decision, every word I speak, and let it begin in me.

In Jesus' Name, Amen.

CHAPTER 13
Cultivating Belonging and Honor
in Every Workplace

The Transforming Power of Belonging and Honor

When people genuinely feel they belong, when they know they are seen, valued, and honored for who they are, not just what they do, something powerful begins to unfold.

They show up with their whole hearts. They contribute with creativity and conviction. They stay when things get hard, not out of obligation, but because they know they matter. And they help others rise, too.

Belonging and honor are not fluffy ideals or feel-good slogans. They are spiritual principles with eternal weight. They are critical, divine strategies.

When woven into the fabric of a workplace, belonging and honor create cultures where potential is unlocked, trust is multiplied, and broken pieces become building blocks for something stronger. People stop competing and start collaborating. They stop hiding and start healing.

Romans 12:10 (ESV) gives us a radical call: "Love one another with brotherly affection. Outdo one another in showing honor."

What if our workplaces looked like that? What if leaders weren't just focused on performance, but on outdoing one another in honor? What if team meetings were infused with mutual respect, and every hallway, office, or Zoom room became a place where people were reminded they matter?

When organizations cultivate this kind of culture, where

belonging is nurtured and honor is practiced, something greater than profit is produced. Lives are restored. Futures are redeemed. Whole communities begin to shift.

This is how we build not just strong companies, but thriving Kingdom ecosystems where purpose is awakened, people are loved well, and the workplace becomes one of the most powerful places of transformation on earth.

Why Belonging and Honor Aren't Optional, They're Essential

Today's employees are seeking far more than a paycheck. They're longing for a place where they belong. A purpose they can believe in. A community they can grow with. A mission that aligns with their heart. And when belonging and honor are missing, something begins to break.

Workplaces become transactional, cold, mechanical, impersonal. Or they become toxic, drained by comparison, distrust, and silent disappointment.

Talented people start to feel invisible. Creativity withers in the shadows of insecurity. Retention drops, not because people aren't capable, but because they no longer feel seen. Morale quietly erodes until even the most passionate efforts collapse under unspoken discouragement.

But when belonging and honor are embedded into a team's DNA, when they aren't just values on a wall but lived-out virtues, everything changes.

Teams thrive. Creativity explodes. Loyalty deepens. Healing, joy, and growth become the new normal. This isn't wishful thinking; it's biblical design.

Now you {collectively} are Christ's body, and individually {you are} members of it {each with his own special purpose and function}.
— 1 Corinthians 12:27 AMP

Every person matters. Every voice matters. Every gift matters. And every soul deserves to be seen, celebrated, and honored.

Belonging and honor aren't optional extras. They are the atmosphere in which people become who God created them to be, and where workplaces are transformed into environments that don't just produce…They restore.

How to Cultivate Belonging in Every Workplace

1. Create an Inclusive Culture

Inclusion is not simply about diverse hiring practices; it's about creating spaces where every voice is heard, valued, and respected. It's about ensuring that every heart feels at home.

Practical Actions:

- Involve diverse employees meaningfully in decision-making, not just in appearance.
- Host regular "listening sessions" where employees can speak freely without fear.
- Take visible, tangible action on feedback received.

Empowerment Coaching Tip: Start meetings with a *"Voice Round,"* inviting everyone to share one thought or insight before addressing the agenda.

2. Foster Open Communication

Communication is the oxygen of belonging. When words flow freely, upward, downward, and sideways, people breathe easier and dream bigger.

Practical Actions:

- Normalize feedback conversations, both giving and receiving.
- Train managers to listen more than they speak.
- Ask often: *"What are we not talking about that we should be?"*

Biblical Wisdom:

Anxiety in a man's heart weighs it down, but a good (encouraging) word makes it glad. — Proverbs 12:25, AMP.

3. Encourage Meaningful Engagement

Engagement doesn't just happen. It blooms when people know they matter beyond what they produce.

Practical Actions:

- Give employees actual ownership over projects and ideas.
- Celebrate initiative and heart, not just outcomes.
- Create mentorship pipelines for growth at every level.

4. Provide Equal Opportunities

Belonging means leveling the playing field so that every dreamer has a fair shot at thriving.

Practical Actions:

- Regularly audit promotion and advancement prac-

tices for equity and fairness.
- Provide leadership development opportunities across demographics, backgrounds, and roles.
- Celebrate different learning styles, problem-solving approaches, and talents.

5. Empower Idea Sharing and Feedback

People feel like they belong when their voices carry weight.

Empowerment Coaching Tip: Host regular *"Idea Huddles"*, short, dynamic team gatherings focused purely on brainstorming without judgment.

How to Cultivate Honor in Every Workplace

1. Define and Live Out Clear Values

A thriving culture grows from the seeds of what is celebrated and corrected. Honor must be visible, vocal, and vibrantly alive in daily decisions.

Practical Actions:

- Define core organizational values with input from all levels.
- Display them proudly.
- Practice them faithfully, especially when it costs.

Biblical Wisdom:

But now the Lord declares, "Far be it from Me—for those who honor Me I will honor, and those who despise Me will be insignifi-

cant and contemptible. " — *1 Samuel 2:30, AMP.*

2. Embrace Feedback as Growth

Feedback is not failure; it is fertilizer for the flourishing of purpose.

Practical Actions:

- Make giving and receiving feedback a natural rhythm, not a rare event.
- Celebrate feedback moments as growth opportunities.

3. Recognize and Celebrate Accomplishments

Honor grows where appreciation is generously sown.

Practical Actions:

- Celebrate both the big wins and the small, daily victories.
- Recognize teamwork, character, effort, and heart, not just results.
- Establish *"Shout Out Fridays"* to spotlight kindness, collaboration, and creativity.

Empowerment Coaching Tip: Take time for handwritten notes of encouragement. A personal word spoken in love can change a career, even a life.

4. Foster Two-Way Communication

Honor is shown by listening to the dreams, fears, and

insights of others. Invite employees into the conversations that shape the future.

How Leaders Build Belonging and Honor

- *Be Present:* Leadership presence is pastoral, not positional, in giving wisdom and guidance.
- *Honor First:* Set the emotional tone by honoring others before expecting honor in return.
- *Serve, Then Lead:* Greatness flows from servanthood. (Mark 10:43-45)
- *Protect Psychological Safety:* Build spaces where authenticity, mistakes, and growth are not just tolerated, but celebrated.
- *Create Rituals of Belonging:* birthdays, gratitude circles, vision retreats all rhythmically celebrate the heartbeats of the community.

Biblical Models of Belonging and Honor

Scripture offers us a radically different model rooted in belonging and honor in a world that often prizes power over people and performance over presence. These aren't soft, sentimental values. They are *Kingdom principles.* They build trust, restore dignity, and create communities (workplaces included) where people can flourish in their God-given identity and purpose.

Let's look at how **three biblical leaders** modeled belonging and honor in transformational ways.

1. Jesus: The Welcomer of the Outcast (Luke 15:1–2)

Throughout His ministry, Jesus consistently broke cultural and religious norms to restore dignity to those the world had rejected. He sat with tax collectors, healed lepers, and protected the woman caught in adultery. He didn't just include the outcast, He made them feel cherished.

In Luke 15, when religious leaders criticized Him for welcoming "sinners," Jesus told the story of the lost sheep, the lost coin, and the prodigal son, not to defend Himself, but to show that Heaven rejoices when the overlooked are brought back into belonging.

Restorers do the same. We go out of our way to see the unseen, hear the unheard, and welcome the overlooked. Whether it's the quiet employee in the corner, the new hire from a different background, or the team member recovering from failure, every person deserves to know: *You belong.*

2. David: The King Who Honored His Enemy (1 Samuel 24:10–12)

David had every reason to dishonor Saul. Saul was jealous. He was unstable. He tried to kill David multiple times. Yet, when David had the perfect opportunity to take Saul's life in the cave, he didn't. Why? Because David understood that honor isn't about whether someone deserves it, it's about your character before God.

David honored Saul's position as king, even as he distanced himself from Saul's behavior. His restraint and reverence for God's anointed and preserved not only his future, but also his integrity.

Restorers lead this way. We rise higher in workplaces where backbiting, gossip, and disrespect are common. We speak with dignity. We disagree with grace. We honor the image of God in every person, even those we find difficult.

3. Paul: The Champion of Every Gift (1 Corinthians 12:4–6)

Paul had an elite education and spiritual authority, but didn't use it to elevate himself. Instead, he wrote passionately about the unique gifts *of every believer* in the Body of Christ. In 1 Corinthians 12, he emphasized that the hand cannot say to the eye, "I don't need you." Every part is essential. Every voice matters.

He was not intimidated by diversity; he celebrated it. Restorers do the same. We recognize that strength lies not in uniformity but in unity. We intentionally create workplace cultures where differences in race, age, gender, personality, and skill are not just tolerated but treasured.

We build teams where every person knows: I matter here. My contribution is valued. I don't have to compete to belong.

Your Call to Lead with Belonging and Honor

You, dear reader, are called to follow in their footsteps. To create a culture of radical inclusion. To honor even when it's hard. To champion the gifts in others, even when they outshine yours. This is what Restorers do. This is how we turn workplaces into centers of healing, hope, and unity.

And it starts with the decision:

- To *lead* like Jesus.
- To *honor* like David.
- To *celebrate* like Paul.

You were born to build a culture where every heart feels safe, seen, and significant. True leadership doesn't just manage tasks; it ministers to hearts.

Ways to Cultivate Belonging and Honor

Team Reflection Prompts:

Use these questions in team meetings, one-on-ones, or personal journaling to foster deeper awareness:

- When was the last time you truly felt like you belonged at work?
- What contributed to that feeling?
- Have you ever felt overlooked or undervalued on this team?
- What would have helped restore that moment?
- Who on our team consistently models honor in the way they treat others?
- What do they do that stands out?
- What's one slight shift we could make as a team to ensure people feel more seen, safe, and celebrated here?
- How might God be calling you personally to create more belonging in this environment?

Practical Ways to Cultivate Belonging & Honor

1. *Call out the gold in others.* Publicly acknowledge people's efforts, not just results. Speak to their character, not just their contributions.

2. *Create space for every voice.* In meetings, actively invite input from quieter team members. Let diversity of thought be seen as strength, not friction.

3. *Celebrate both wins and growth.* Honor not just milestones, but personal growth, perseverance, and transformation along the journey.

4. *Listen, without agenda.* Honor people by offering your full presence. Make space for real, honest conversations, especially when feedback is hard.

5. *Learn people's stories.* Ask about someone's background, culture, or dreams. You can't honor what you don't understand.

6. *Make belonging visible.* Use inclusive language. Celebrate birthdays, life events, and work anniversaries. Let people see themselves reflected in your culture.

7. *Give honor freely, not conditionally.* You don't have to agree with someone to honor them. Lead with respect, even when it's difficult.

8. *Protect others' dignity behind closed doors.* Speak about teammates in private with the same respect you'd give in public. Integrity builds safety.

Spiritual Reminder:

Be devoted to one another in love. Honor one another above yourselves. — Romans 12:10, NIV

When honor becomes your culture, belonging becomes your atmosphere, and healing becomes your legacy.

Reflection Questions

1. How well does my current workplace or team cultivate true belonging?
2. How intentionally do I honor the people around me?
3. What one step can I take this week to build more belonging and honor into my leadership?

Workplace Healing Action Steps

- Publicly honor someone for who they are this week, not just what they do.

- Start your next team meeting with a belonging prompt: *"What makes you feel seen and valued at work?"*
- Review your organization's stated values. Are they truly visible, lived, and celebrated?

Destiny Declarations

Speak these aloud in faith:

- *Through Christ, I create spaces where every heart feels seen, valued, and empowered.*
- *I am a builder of belonging and a sower of honor.*
- *My leadership reflects the very heart of God: love, dignity, and respect for every soul.*

Workplace Restoration Toolkit (Appendix Reference)

In the Appendix, you'll find:

- *Belonging Culture Checklist*
- *Sample Employee Recognition Templates*
- *Belonging & Honor Leadership Reflection Guide*

(See Appendix A for practical next steps to create a workplace where belonging and honor aren't just ideals but the daily reality.)

Prayer: Lord, Let Belonging and Honor Begin With Me

Gracious God,

You are the One who welcomes every soul, sees what others overlook, calls the forgotten by name, and crowns the humble with glory. In Your presence, no one is invisible. No one is disposable. No one is without purpose. And today,

I ask You, make me that kind of leader.

Lord, help me create spaces where belonging is not earned but given freely. Let every person I encounter feel seen, known, and valued, not for their output but for their heart, journey, and divine design. Break any pride, prejudice, or performance-driven mindset in me that causes others to shrink when You've called them to rise.

Teach me to outdo others in showing honor; to speak life, not labels… to lift, not tear down… to celebrate, not compete. Let my words be healing. Let my presence carry peace. Let my leadership reflect the heart of Heaven.

Forgive me, Lord, for every time I've been too busy to notice someone's pain, too focused on results to recognize someone's worth, or too fearful to stand up for the overlooked. I surrender those moments to You. Heal what I've missed. Restore what I've damaged, and renew in me a vision for what Your Kingdom culture could look like at work.

Father, give me eyes like Jesus to welcome the outcast. Give me humility like David to honor even those who've wounded me. Give me Paul's encouragement to champion every gift, every voice, and every story.

Let belonging and honor start with me. Let them flow from my heart, saturate my words, and shape the culture I help create.

I declare:

- *I am a vessel of honor.*
- *I am a cultivator of belonging.*
- *Through Christ, I create spaces where every person knows they matter and every gift is celebrated.*

May my leadership invite Your presence. May my team become a reflection of Heaven. And may my workplace become a place where destinies are awakened and healing begins.

In Jesus' Name, Amen.

PART V:
UNLOCKING DESTINY AND PROFIT

CHAPTER 14

From Workplace to World-Changer:
How Small Acts Transform Cultures

You don't need a title, a corner office, or your name on the door to be a world-changer. You simply need a willing heart and a courageous spirit.

Real transformation doesn't always come with applause or promotion; it often begins in quiet decisions made with conviction. It happens one conversation at a time. One act of integrity at a time. One moment of kindness, humility, or truth spoken in love.

Your workplace is more than a place where you earn a paycheck. It is holy ground. It's your assignment. It's part of your calling.

You were placed there by God on purpose and for a purpose, not just to complete tasks, but to carry His light, His love, and His healing into every space you touch.

When you show up healed, whole, and led by the Spirit, you shift atmospheres. You spark transformation. You don't just impact productivity, you awaken purpose in yourself and in others.

As Colossians 3:23, AMP reminds us: "Whatever you do [whatever your task may be], work from the soul [that is, put in your very best effort], as [something done] for the Lord and not for men."

When you lead, work, and serve from a place of spiritual alignment, your daily efforts become eternal investments. And the ripple effect? It's far greater than you can imagine.

This isn't just work. This is worship. This is purpose in

motion. This is your mission field. And you, right where you are, are a Restorer.

Unlocking Destiny in the Workplace

Destiny doesn't just happen; it's revealed through faithful stewardship, one decision at a time. It's not found in waiting for the perfect opportunity; it's unlocked when we show up with intention, excellence, and a heart ready to serve.

Your destiny begins where you are, right now, in the daily choices you make, the attitude you bring, and the atmosphere you help create. Don't wait for a title or permission to lead. Lead by example. Lead by kindness. Lead by filling the gaps no one else sees.

Ask clarifying questions in meetings and volunteer for projects that stretch you. Speak life into conversations that feel heavy. What you do may seem small, but in the Kingdom, small seeds unlock eternal harvests.

Destiny also grows through a commitment to learning. Lifelong learners outlast trends, outgrow limitations, and lift others as they rise. Read the books. Take the workshop. Ask for feedback. Seek mentors who don't just affirm you, but refine you.

And never underestimate the power of showing up, on time, with integrity, and with your whole heart. Quiet excellence speaks louder than flashy performance. Destiny is drawn to faithfulness. It flows through consistency. It multiplies through character.

But perhaps most profoundly, destiny unfolds in relationship. God often releases our next assignment through divine connections: people who see us, challenge us, and open doors we could never force open on our own. So prioritize people. Build trust. Listen deeply. Encourage generously. Make it a habit to see the gold in others, even when stress tries to blind you. And above all, stay grateful.

Gratitude shifts atmospheres faster than any strategy. Say thank you often, out loud and in writing. Appreciate the small wins. Celebrate the small beginnings. A grateful heart is a magnet for miracles.

Your destiny won't be unlocked by accident. It will be unlocked by daily partnership with God, with people, and with purpose.

Controlling Your Destiny at Work and in Life

You are not powerless. You are not at the mercy of your workplace, your boss, your past, or your current challenges. You are not a victim of circumstance; you are a steward of influence.

Your destiny isn't something that randomly finds you; it's something you co-labor with God to uncover and walk out, step by step, decision by decision.

That begins with taking radical responsibility, not just for your workload, but also for your attitude, mindset, and growth. Stop waiting for someone else to create a better environment. Be the one who shifts the atmosphere. Show up with hope where others are cynical. Bring order where there's chaos. Extend grace where there's tension. You may not be able to control everything around you, but you can absolutely control what flows from within you.

Start asking:

- "What is this challenge trying to teach me?"
- "How is God stretching me through this?"
- "What fruit does He want to produce in me here, right now?"

Reframe every frustration as a training ground. Your current pressure might be preparing you for a level of impact that comfort could never produce.

And don't try to do it alone. Build a support network, people who see your potential, who speak truth, who sharpen your edges without dulling your worth. Proverbs 27:17 reminds us, "As iron sharpens iron, so one person sharpens another."

Let feedback be your fertilizer. Don't receive correction as rejection. Receive it as preparation. Ask for it. Listen with humility. Apply it with boldness.

Growth is your responsibility, and your superpower. You don't need perfection to walk in destiny. You need hunger, humility, and a willingness to rise when it's easier to retreat. So rise.

Not someday. Not when it gets easier. Now. Right where you are. With what you have. Because when you take ownership of your attitude, your actions, and your assignment, destiny doesn't delay. It accelerates.

Ways to Take Ownership of Your Destiny

1. **Show Up With Purpose:** Don't just clock in, check in. Every day, ask: "What's my *why* today?" Let purpose, not pressure, lead your actions.

2. **Shift From Complaining to Creating:** Instead of rehearsing what's broken, ask, "What can I build here? What do I have the power to influence?" Be the solution.

3. **Take Initiative:** Don't wait to be asked. Step into opportunities. Offer help. Start the project. Lead the conversation. Destiny responds to movement.

4. **Embrace Growth Over Comfort:** Push past what's familiar. Sign up for the course. Ask for feedback. Say yes to what stretches you, even if it scares you.

5. Surround Yourself With Sharpeners: Seek out mentors, coaches, and peers who challenge and inspire you. Let them speak truth, even when it stings.

6. Own Your Energy: Guard your thoughts. Rest when needed. Set boundaries. Fuel your day with faith, not frustration.

7. Act With Excellence, Even Unseen: Do your best not because someone's watching, but because you're called. Excellence in the unseen builds influence in the seen.

8. Stay Grateful and Expectant: Gratitude shifts the atmosphere. Expectancy activates your faith. Thank God for where you are, and trust Him for where you're going.

Profiting from Destiny in the Workplace

True profit isn't just measured in paychecks or promotions. It's measured in the lives you impact, the trust you build, the growth you embrace, and the legacy you leave behind.

You profit when your skill is seasoned with integrity, when excellence becomes your standard, not to impress others, but to honor God and steward what He's placed in your hands. You profit when you choose growth over comfort, courage over convenience, and purpose over performance.

Destiny pays dividends when you consistently show up with a teachable spirit and a heart willing to stretch. Set bold, God-inspired goals each year, not just for what you want to achieve, but for who you want to become. Seek out opportunities to serve, mentor, lead, and make room for others to rise with you.

Challenges? Don't resist them. Welcome them as divine training grounds. Each obstacle you overcome increases your capacity for greater influence, deeper wisdom, and a higher purpose.

This kind of profit is spiritual. It's relational. It's generational. And best of all, it's eternal.

Becoming a World-Changer Through Small Acts

You don't need a spotlight to make a difference. You don't need a stage, a title, or a platform. Some of the greatest world-changers are those who quietly sow seeds of kindness, faithfulness, and integrity behind the scenes, day after day, choice after choice.

Every encouraging word you speak, every patient response you give, every moment you choose to listen instead of rushing, these are not small things. They are kingdom acts with ripple effects that stretch far beyond what you can see.

Offer help before it's asked for. Write thank-you notes that remind someone they matter. Celebrate others' strengths out loud, without competition, without envy. Give your coworkers the gift of your full attention, your compassion, your belief in them.

Most of all, stay the course. Continue showing up with kindness even when it's not reciprocated. Keep choosing humility when pride would be easier. Keep doing good even when it feels like no one notices because Heaven does.

Scripture promises us in Galatians 6:9, "Let us not grow weary in doing good, for at the proper time we will reap a harvest if we do not give up." Every brave, faithful choice you make today plants seeds for someone else's healing tomorrow.

Your workplace isn't just where you clock in and out. It's your mission field. It's your launching pad. And it may very well be the place where someone else's life is transformed because you dared to lead with love, integrity, and hope.

Don't underestimate the small. That's where world-changers are born.

Reflection Questions:

1. What small act of courage, kindness, or excellence could I start doing daily in my workplace?
2. Where have I been waiting for change, instead of becoming the change?
3. How is God calling me to steward my workplace assignment more intentionally this season?

Workplace Healing Action Steps

- Write down one way you will show up as a "world-changer" in your workplace this week, even in small, unseen ways.
- Offer tangible encouragement to at least one colleague each day this week.
- Identify a new project, opportunity, or skill you can say "yes" to that will stretch you into your next level of destiny.

Destiny Declarations:

Speak these boldly in faith:

- *Through Christ, I am a world-changer right where I am planted.*
- *I unleash destinies through my faithfulness, kindness, and courage.*
- *I steward my workplace as my assignment, training ground, and mission field.*

Workplace Restoration Toolkit (Appendix Reference):

In the Appendix, you'll find practical tools to help you activate your world-changing assignment immediately:

- *Small Acts, Big Impact Challenge Guide*
- *Daily World-Changer Reflection Journal*
- *Personal Destiny Activation Checklist*

(See Appendix A: Workplace Restoration Toolkit.)

Prayer: Lord, Use Me to Change the World Right Where I Am

Heavenly Father,

Thank You for reminding me that I don't need a platform, a title, or applause to make a difference; I just need a surrendered heart. Right here, in the ordinary rhythm of my workday, You have placed me on sacred ground. This is not just a job; it is a Kingdom assignment.

Lord, awaken my spirit to the opportunities all around me. Help me see my workplace through Your eyes, not just as a place of production but a place of purpose. Teach me to lead with love in small ways: a kind word, a helping hand, a listening ear. Remind me that even the smallest act of obedience can ripple through eternity.

Fill me with courage to step forward when I want to shrink back. Let me bring Your peace into tense conversations, Your excellence into mundane tasks, and Your compassion into every relationship. May my faithfulness, even in what feels unnoticed, be a light that draws others to You.

When I grow weary, renew my strength. When I feel unseen, remind me that You see every seed I sow. When I doubt my impact, anchor me in Your promise: I will reap in due season if I don't give up.

Lord, make me a Restorer, a world-changer, not through grand gestures, but through daily faithfulness. Let my presence shift atmospheres. Let my work glorify You. Let my life point to something greater.

I offer You my hands, my heart, and this workplace. Do what only You can do.

In Jesus' Name, Amen.

CHAPTER 15

Designing Organizations That
Heal and Prosper

Envisioning a Healed and Whole Workplace

Imagine this: a workplace where people don't merely show up to survive the day, but where they heal from what life has broken, grow into who they're meant to be, and flourish in ways that touch *both earth and eternity.*

Picture an organization where integrity is the norm, not the exception. Where empathy flows through every meeting, every decision, and every conversation. Where prosperity is measured not only by profits, but by purpose fulfilled, relationships strengthened, and lives restored.

This is not a fantasy. This is not just wishful thinking. This is the future God is inviting us to build together.

Workplaces can be more than engines for output and performance. They can be platforms for healing, wholeness, and destiny. They can become sacred spaces where gifts are discovered, trust is restored, and hearts come alive again. It is possible. And it starts with wisdom. God's wisdom.

Proverbs 24:3–4 tells us:

Through {skillful and godly} wisdom a house {a life, a home, a family} is built, and by understanding it is established {on a sound and good foundation}, and by knowledge its rooms are filled with all precious and pleasant riches. — Proverbs 24:3–4, AMP

This applies to your workplace, too. Healthy, healing

organizations don't appear by accident. *They are intentionally designed.* They're built by leaders, like you, who are willing to embrace God's wisdom, lead with love, and lay down ego for the sake of something greater.

If your workplace feels toxic, burned out, chaotic, or empty, it doesn't have to stay that way. The atmosphere can shift. The culture can change. Restoration is possible. And it begins with you.

You are not just here to survive work. You are here to transform it.

What Could a Healed Workplace Look Like for You?

Take a moment. Breathe. Step away from the stress, noise, and demands that may fill your day, and imagine what's possible.

What if healing didn't have to wait for the next job, a new boss, or a company-wide initiative? What if it could begin with you, right where you are?

Let these questions guide your vision:

- What would it feel like to wake up and not dread the day ahead? Would peace greet you instead of pressure? Would you walk into work lighter, more grounded, more you?
- What kind of conversations would fill your day if trust and honor were the norm? Would feedback feel safe? Would collaboration flow freely? Would hard conversations lead to a deeper connection, rather than disconnection?
- What would it be like to be led by someone who saw your potential and your pain, and valued both? Would you grow in confidence? Would your gifts

multiply? Would your joy return?

- If you're the leader, how would it change your team to create an atmosphere of belonging and grace? Would burnout begin to lift? Would creativity rise? Would loyalty deepen?
- How would it feel to know that your presence at work helps others feel seen, safe, and empowered? What kind of ripple effects might that spark, in their families, in their faith, in their futures?
- What might God be inviting you to build, heal, or restore in the environment you spend so much of your life in?

Now ask yourself: What's one small shift I can make this week to begin cultivating a healing atmosphere, in my words, my attitude, my leadership, or my choices?

Write it down. Pray over it. Act on it. Healing doesn't require permission. It begins with intention.

You are not powerless here. You are positioned. You are not just clocking in. You are carrying light. You are not waiting for change. You are becoming it.

Let your workplace become a testimony, not just of excellence, but of healing, transformation, and Kingdom purpose in action.

How to Create Workplaces That Foster Healing

Healing workplaces don't just care about what people produce; they care about who people are. In these environments, the whole person is honored: heart, mind, body, soul, and spirit. People aren't treated as machines or titles, but as humans with dreams, challenges, emotions, and purpose.

When healing becomes part of the workplace culture, people begin to *breathe* easier. They feel seen, heard, valued, and empowered, not just to work harder, but to grow, rise, and overcome. In healing workplaces, encouragement isn't a once-a-year morale booster. It's a daily rhythm, a way of life.

It's in the hallway conversations that uplift. The meetings that make space for new voices. The leaders who ask, *"How are you really doing?"* and pause to listen. It's in the way feedback is delivered, with honesty and grace. And how failures are handled, with compassion and growth, not shame.

Healing organizations don't just manage people. They build them. They create space for vulnerability, emotional safety, and spiritual strength to take root. These are the kind of workplaces where hope lives, where it's safe to bring your whole self to the table, knowing you won't be diminished for being human.

As Scripture reminds us:

Therefore encourage and comfort one another and build up one another, just as you are doing. — *1 Thessalonians 5:11, AMP*

Healing doesn't happen in one day, but it begins with one decision: To lead with compassion, to speak life, to create an atmosphere where people can be real, grow deep, and flourish for the long haul.

When workplaces are built on encouragement, everything changes: retention, morale, creativity, trust, and most of all, the hearts and futures of the people who walk through the doors every day.

Practical Strategies for Cultivating Healing Environments

Healing starts by cultivating empathy at every level of leadership and team dynamics. Empathy transforms tension into trust, and trust into unshakable unity. Organizations must invest in emotional intelligence training and compassionate listening skills so that leaders and employees can truly see one another beyond tasks and titles.

Healing environments must also tend to the whole person by providing resources for mental, physical, and spiritual well-being. Counseling access, stress management programs, fitness initiatives, and wellness workshops should be normalized, not stigmatized.

Communication must flow openly and safely, offering multiple feedback channels so every voice can be heard without fear. Leaders must also model healing behaviors, visibly practicing healthy boundaries, self-care, emotional resilience, and kindness, not as exceptions, but as everyday examples.

Encouragement Practices That Heal

These simple, *intentional actions* can transform the atmosphere of your workplace from weary to life-giving:

1. Start Meetings with Affirmation

Begin team meetings by highlighting something good. Celebrate a win, acknowledge someone's effort, or share a story that uplifts the group. Starting with encouragement sets the emotional tone.

2. Speak Life Daily

Look for opportunities to speak words that build, not just correct. A sincere *"I appreciate you," "You handled that well,"* or *"You made a difference today"* can shift someone's whole mindset.

3. Write Personal Notes

Take time to send handwritten thank-you notes or short messages of encouragement. It's a small gesture with a lasting impact, especially in a world that's increasingly digital and disconnected.

4. Practice Public Praise, Private Correction

Affirm team members in front of others whenever possible. Celebrate their character, not just their performance. Handle mistakes privately with grace and clarity, not shame or blame.

5. Create Safe Check-In Spaces

Make space for authentic check-ins, whether during one-on-ones, morning huddles, or casual breaks. Ask, *"What support do you need this week?"* or *"How's your heart?"* and really listen.

6. Celebrate Progress, Not Just Perfection

Encouragement thrives when we acknowledge growth, even small steps forward. Don't wait for a perfect result. Celebrate consistency, courage, and effort.

7. Empower Peer Encouragement

Create a culture where teammates cheer each other on. Introduce tools like *"encouragement boards,"* shout-outs, or team rituals where peers can uplift one another.

8. Call Out Potential

Don't just recognize what people do, speak to who they're becoming. Say things like, *"I see a leader in you,"* or *"You have a gift for empathy."* This helps people rise into their purpose.

9. Model Encouragement from the Top Down

Leaders set the tone. If you're in leadership, your words create the atmosphere. Be intentional, consistent, and authentic in speaking life over your team.

10. Anchor Encouragement in God's Truth

Share scriptures or biblical truths (when appropriate) that remind people of their value and identity. Speak words that align with God's view of them, not just their role. This is never about pushing your beliefs on others, but about sharing the truth and words of encouragement that have encouraged and guided you (again, when appropriate).

Designing Organizations That Promote Workplace Healing

Healing doesn't happen by chance; *it happens by design.* If we're serious about transforming workplace culture, we must move beyond slogans and start shaping systems that reflect the values we preach.

Creating a healing organization requires more than kindness; it calls for courage, intentionality, and a willingness to reimagine how work is done from the inside out.

Healing cultures are built when restoration is not just encouraged, but embedded into the organization's structure and the way it operates.

That means implementing policies that protect and uplift people, not just productivity. **Organizations that value healing:**

- Offer flexible work schedules that honor life outside of work.
- Provide paid mental health days that acknowledge emotional well-being as essential, not optional.
- Enforce strong, zero-tolerance policies against harassment, discrimination, and toxic behavior.
- Normalize vacation, rest, and unplugging, without guilt or penalty.

Wellness is not a "perk"; it's a strategy. **Forward-thinking organizations incentivize wholeness through:**

- Wellness and gratitude challenges
- Retreats or renewal days
- Access to counselors, coaches, or wellness apps
- Resources that prioritize emotional and spiritual health alongside performance

Leaders set the tone. **Healing** can't just be aspirational; **it must be operationalized.** That looks like:

- Clear communication boundaries, such as "no after-hours emails" or designated "quiet hours"
- Modeling Sabbath rhythms of rest, not hustle, and honoring the pace of grace
- Creating safe physical or digital spaces where team members can pause, breathe, pray, or reflect, because margin is where restoration begins.

Ultimately, compassion must become a leadership discipline, not just a response to crisis. Healing is shown not only in big gestures, but in daily choices: how we listen, how we correct, how we support, and how we lead.

When policies align with purpose and systems support the soul, workplaces begin to reflect the heart of God. And when the workplace becomes a place of healing, lives are changed far beyond the walls of the office.

Healing Policies & Practices That Transform Organizations

Creating a healing workplace isn't just about atmosphere; it's about *action.* The following policies and practices serve as a blueprint for embedding healing into the everyday rhythms of your organization:

1. Prioritize Mental and Emotional Health

- Offer paid mental health days without stigma or penalty.
- Provide access to counseling, coaching, or Employee Assistance Programs (EAPs).
- Host quarterly emotional wellness check-ins or retreats.
- Incorporate grief support or trauma-informed care resources when needed.

2. Protect Time and Energy

- Enforce "no after-hours communication" policies.
- Respect vacation and time off as essential, not extra.
- Encourage Sabbath rhythms: promote unplugged weekends, rest days, and soul care.

- Create buffer space in calendars: schedule "no meeting" blocks or margin days.

3. Build Safe, Restorative Environments

- Designate quiet rooms, prayer spaces, or reflection corners.
- Create wellness zones or break areas that promote relaxation and creativity.
- Use virtual "pause" spaces (wellness Zoom rooms) for remote teams.
- Allow for flexible work locations when possible.

4. Promote Psychological Safety

- Train leaders in empathy-based communication and trauma-informed leadership.
- Encourage employees to speak up without fear of retaliation or dismissal.
- Reward honesty, humility, and thoughtful risk-taking.
- Normalize feedback as a gift, not a threat.

5. Lead by Example

- Have leaders model rest, humility, and emotional intelligence.
- Address mistakes with grace and accountability, not shame.
- Show up with consistency, fairness, and integrity in decision-making.
- Start meetings with moments of gratitude, prayer, or encouragement.

6. Celebrate Wholeness, Not Just Hustle

- Recognize character and growth, not only results.
- Celebrate progress over perfection.
- Implement *"wholeness wins" awards* for emotional, spiritual, or relational breakthroughs.
- Create mentorship structures that nurture the person, not just the performer.

Healing cultures are created intentionally, one policy, one decision, one person at a time. When organizations make space for wholeness, employees bring their best, not just their skills, but their hearts, their hope, and their healing.

Designing Workplaces That Prosper Ethically

According to God's standards, true prosperity is holistic. It includes financial health, but it's built on righteousness, transparency, justice, and love. Prospering unethically is never success; *it's a delayed collapse.*

Healing organizations must first create a culture of integrity, where ethical guidelines are clearly defined, taught, and lived. Dishonesty, favoritism, and corruption must be addressed quickly and consistently. Ethical decision-making should be celebrated even when costly because, as Proverbs 28:6 reminds us, "Better is a poor man who walks in his integrity than a rich man who is crooked in his ways."

Ethical leadership must be modeled consistently by those at the top, with leaders holding themselves accountable first. Training programs should equip everyone, from interns to executives, to view ethics not as compliance, but as a calling. Organizations must also ensure that concerns can be raised without retaliation and that mistakes can be redeemed, not hidden.

Better is the poor who walks in his integrity than he who is crooked and two-faced though he is rich. — *Proverbs 28:6, AMP*

Key Systems for Building Healing and Ethical Prosperity

Behind every thriving, healing workplace is a foundation of healthy systems: structures that quietly shape the culture, reinforce values, and either promote well-being or erode it over time. If we're serious about creating environments where people not only perform but also prosper, emotionally, spiritually, and ethically, we must examine the systems we build, inherit, or tolerate.

Hiring Systems: Every hire is a culture decision. Skills can be taught, but character can't be faked for long. Healing organizations hire people not only for what they can do, but for who they are. They seek alignment with core values, emotional maturity, humility, and a heart to grow alongside the team. They ask: *"Will this person contribute to the atmosphere of honor we're building?"*

Onboarding Systems: First impressions become lasting frameworks. Onboarding shouldn't just be about policies and procedures; it should immerse new team members into the heart, mission, and why of the organization. Healing workplaces don't just assign tasks; they invite people into purpose. They help new hires feel seen, connected, and essential from day one.

Communication Systems: Words shape worlds. A healthy workplace normalizes clear, kind, and consistent communication. Gratitude isn't an afterthought; it's embedded. Feedback isn't feared; it's expected and welcomed. Transparency flows from the top down, building trust and eliminating confusion. Regular rhythms of check-ins, listening sessions, and cross-team conversations keep the culture honest and alive.

Recognition Systems: What gets celebrated gets repeated. Too often, companies only recognize outcomes, such as sales, statistics, and numbers. But healing organizations know that how people lead, love, and show up matters just as much as what they accomplish. They celebrate character: courage, empathy, faithfulness, innovation, and integrity. They spotlight people who elevate others and embody the mission, not just those who hit Key Performance Indicators (KPIs).

Correction and Accountability Systems: Correction should never crush dignity. Healthy systems know how to hold people accountable while separating identity from behavior. Mistakes are addressed with truth and grace. The goal isn't shame; it's restoration. These systems model what it looks like to correct in love, creating space for growth rather than fear.

Wellness and Support Systems: Thriving teams require soul care. In healing cultures, wellness isn't a perk; it's a pillar of health. Mental health, emotional safety, physical rest, and spiritual nourishment are all seen as essential to productivity and longevity.

Systems might include access to coaching or counseling, built-in Sabbath rhythms, wellness stipends, team retreats, or soul care check-ins. Because healed people build healthy workplaces, and burnout is not a badge of honor.

Organizations that build these systems don't just retain talent; they release destiny. They become known not only for what they produce, but for how they care, how they restore, and how they empower every life they touch.

Biblical Models for Healing and Prosperous Leadership

We are not without guidance. In His infinite wisdom, God has already laid out divine blueprints for healing, restorative, and thriving leadership. These are not just stories from long ago; they are sacred strategies, timeless leadership frameworks, and spiritual roadmaps we are invited to walk out today.

1. Nehemiah: The Rebuilder with Vision and Prayer

Nehemiah didn't rebuild the broken walls of Jerusalem alone. He rallied people from all walks of life to rise, restore, and take ownership of their part. He prayed before he moved. He cast vision with clarity. He stayed rooted in divine direction, even amidst opposition and weariness.

Nehemiah teaches us that healing leadership starts with burden and builds with strategy. It requires deep empathy for others and a refusal to let injustice or brokenness go unchecked. As modern leaders, we are called to be like Nehemiah, prayerful planners, courageous communicators, and defenders of the vulnerable.

Coaching Insight: When rebuilding broken systems or teams, begin with prayer, clarify your vision, assign responsibility with trust, and hold the line with accountability rooted in grace.

2. Jesus: The Servant Leader Who Restored Hearts

Jesus didn't come with political power or institutional backing. He came with towels and tears. He knelt, washed feet, ate with outcasts, healed what society rejected, spoke truth with compassion, and offered belonging to those pushed out by culture.

His leadership was love in action. His authority flowed from humility. His power was proven in how He lifted others up, not how He kept them down.

As Restorers, we lead like Jesus when we care more about people than platforms, more about presence than performance. Authentic healing leadership is not afraid to get close to brokenness. It invites people to be seen, known, and restored.

Coaching Insight: The most significant influence you'll ever have is how you love people when they feel unlovable at work, home, and in the hallway. Start there.

3. The Early Church: A Model of Shared Power and Radical Generosity

The book of Acts shows a radical, countercultural community exploding with growth, not because of charisma but Christ-centered connection. They met daily, encouraged continually, gave generously, and led collectively. Everyone mattered. Everyone contributed.

This model challenges hierarchical, transactional leadership. It reveals that unity, shared vision, and emotional safety lead to supernatural momentum. When leaders prioritize belonging, break bread with their people, and give voice to the unheard, organizations flourish from the inside out.

Coaching Insight: Growth is not just about numbers;

it's about depth. If you want a thriving team, build rhythms of relational connection and mutual encouragement into your systems.

Your Invitation to Lead Differently

These are not just inspirational stories; they are spiritual templates for leadership in the 21st century. Whether you're managing a team of two or leading a company of thousands, God is calling you to build what the world cannot: workplaces that heal, communities that prosper, and teams that reflect Heaven.

Nehemiah showed us how to rebuild, Jesus showed us how to restore, and the early church showed us how to thrive together. And now, beloved Restorer...it's your turn.

Reflection Questions

1. Where in my organization (or team) are healing and human flourishing already happening?
2. What systems or habits need to be realigned with God's wisdom and Kingdom values?
3. What is one bold step I can take this quarter to design a more healing, prosperous workplace?

Workplace Healing Action Steps

- Conduct a *"Healing Audit"* to evaluate how well your organization fosters belonging, safety, and purpose.
- Initiate one new practice that supports human flourishing, such as gratitude rituals, flexible scheduling, or leadership development programs.

- Create a Team Covenant or a Culture Manifesto rooted deeply in your organization's core values and Biblical principles.

Destiny Declarations

Declare these boldly over your leadership and organization:

- *Through Christ, I am building workplaces where destinies are discovered, developed, and deployed.*
- *I design cultures that heal hearts, unlock potential, and prosper by Kingdom principles.*
- *Every system I create reflects my God's love, wisdom, and excellence.*

Workplace Restoration Toolkit (Appendix Reference):

In the Appendix, you'll find:

- *Healing Workplace Design Checklist*
- *Sample Ethical Leadership Commitment Templates*
- *Wellness Program Launch Guide*

(See Appendix A: Workplace Restoration Toolkit for practical tools and templates.)

Prayer: Lord, Help Me Design a Healing and Prosperous Workplace

Heavenly Father,

I come before You with gratitude for the sacred assignment of leadership You've placed in my hands. Thank You for entrusting me not just with systems and structures, but with souls. Help me steward this calling with reverence, vision, and compassion.

Lord, awaken in me a more profound wisdom, Your wisdom, that builds foundations of peace, truth, and wholeness in every corner of my workplace. Just as You build houses with wisdom and fill rooms with riches that matter, let my leadership reflect Your divine design.

Teach me to lead like Jesus, with humility, integrity, and love that sees the invisible and lifts the broken. Let my words be healing. Let my decisions be just. Let my heart be tuned to the needs of those You've placed around me.

I pray that the atmosphere I help shape will be one where people feel safe to grow, seen for who they are, and supported as they step into purpose. Let encouragement be our daily language. Let restoration be our rhythm. Let excellence be born from empathy, not ego.

Lord, where there are systems that harm, redeem them. Where there are policies that exclude, revise them. Where hearts are growing weary, revive them.

Make me a Restorer who not only dreams of healing organizations but builds them, brick by brick, with bold faith and compassionate leadership.

I declare that through Christ, I am designing spaces where people are not drained but developed... not overlooked but honored... not just hired but healed. I have got the grace to make these changes.

Let my leadership reflect Heaven. Let my workplace be fertile ground for destinies to bloom. And may every decision I make leave a legacy that honors You.

In Jesus' Name, Amen.

CHAPTER 16

Your Destiny Awaits:
The Workplace Restoration Movement Starts With You

You Are Not Here by Accident

Pause for a moment and consider this: You are not reading these words, and have not come this far in this book, by coincidence. This is a divine appointment.

Right now, yes, in the very workplace where stress is high, where relationships may feel strained, where your impact feels hidden or your efforts overlooked, God has positioned you for a purpose bigger than you realize. You've been sent, not just hired. Placed, not just promoted. And your assignment doesn't begin someday. It begins today.

Even if you feel exhausted. Even if your workplace feels like chaos. Even if you doubt whether you can make a difference at all. You are being called to rise as a Restorer.

A Restorer is not perfect, polished, or powerful by the world's standards. A Restorer is someone who chooses healing over harming, unity over division, and purpose over self-preservation.

You are called to build bridges, even when walls feel safer. You are called to bring healing, even in places marked by years of hurt. You are called to speak life, even in rooms heavy with silence or tension. You are called to embody hope, especially where fear has shaped the culture.

You don't need a title to do this. You don't need a corner office or a promotion. You need a willing heart and a daily *"yes"* to walk in courage, humility, and love.

Maybe your workplace feels like a desert right now, dry, unfruitful, weary. But Isaiah 58:11 offers a promise that still holds true:

The Lord will guide you always; He will satisfy your needs in a sun-scorched land and will strengthen your frame. You will be like a well-watered garden, like a spring whose waters never fail.
— Isaiah 58:11, NIV

This is what happens when you choose to show up healed, whole, and willing:

- You become a wellspring of restoration in dry places.
- You shift atmospheres simply by how you carry yourself.
- You make the invisible Kingdom visible through your leadership, your love, and your integrity.

So don't wait for the culture to change. Become the change. Don't wait for someone else to speak up. Be the voice of healing. Don't hold back your compassion, your wisdom, your light. Let it flow.

Your courage will inspire someone else's. Your consistency will rebuild trust. Your faithfulness will unlock destinies you may never fully see, but Heaven will.

This is your moment. This is your mission. And you are not alone.

How to Reach Your Destiny in the Workplace

The path to destiny is not about giant leaps; it's about small, faithful, courageous steps taken daily. The first step is to define your purpose clearly. Purpose gives you staying power when circumstances feel heavy, unfair, or overwhelming. Without a crystal-clear sense of why you are there, why you show up each day, discouragement can pull you off course.

Take time to prayerfully craft a **Personal Workplace Mission Statement.** Maybe it sounds like this: *"I am here to lead with love, restore with grace, and build a legacy of healing and excellence."* Write it. Declare it. Live by it. As Proverbs 16:3, NIV assures us, "Commit to the Lord whatever you do, and he will establish your plans."

Surrounding yourself with supportive people is just as critical. Destiny rarely unfolds in isolation. It blossoms in the soil of godly relationships. Seek out mentors who believe in you, friends who encourage your walk, and colleagues who value integrity, kindness, and growth.

Connect intentionally to communities, churches, groups, and circles that inspire your spiritual and professional journey. Remember, movements are not built overnight. You don't restore a broken culture with one grand gesture. You rebuild it one courageous, faithful step at a time.

Focus on the *"next faithful step"* instead of being overwhelmed by the staircase you can't see fully yet. God honors small beginnings and small steps taken with a surrendered heart.

You must also cultivate holy resilience, the kind that gets back up again and again without shame.

Setbacks are not signs of failure; they are training for your next assignment. Every challenge you face becomes a stretching season, preparing you for greater capacity. Speak life over yourself daily, as Proverbs 18:21 reminds us: "The tongue has the power of life and death."

Consistency will always beat short bursts of intensity. Stay faithful in the small things and watch God multiply your influence over time.

And yes, be likable, but remain authentic. Being a joy

to work with, choosing encouragement over gossip, positivity over negativity, and patience over frustration will open doors no résumé ever could.

Let your life shine with the fruits of the Spirit, love, joy, peace, patience, kindness, goodness, faithfulness, gentleness, and self-control (Galatians 5:22-23). This is how you become a Restorer people want to follow.

Finally, stay open to learning. Destiny requires humility. Ask for feedback without defensiveness, receive correction with gratitude, and always posture your heart as a student, no matter how much you achieve. *God trusts lifelong learners with lifelong impact.*

How to Restore a Workplace

Restoration starts with addressing the conflicts most people are too afraid to face. Unresolved tension is a silent toxin that destroys cultures from the inside out. Healthy workplaces don't ignore conflict; they resolve it quickly, fairly, and with compassion. Train teams to have courageous conversations and equip leaders to model humility and accountability.

Trust is the next essential ingredient, and it's rebuilt not through words, but through consistent daily behavior. Keep promises. Communicate openly. Apologize when necessary. *Do what you say you will do.* Over time, these small acts rebuild even the most fractured bridges.

A positive culture must also be intentionally cultivated. It grows in the soil of celebration, where acts of kindness, collaboration, excellence, and perseverance are noticed and honored. Celebrate small wins loudly. Make gratitude louder than complaints. Culture is created by what you celebrate, tolerate, and correct; never forget that.

How to Restore a Healthy Emotional Environment

Healing workplaces prioritize emotional well-being just as much as deadlines and deliverables. Teaching emotional intelligence, the ability to recognize, manage, and respond wisely to emotions, is crucial.

Train people to manage their reactions, communicate with empathy, and process stress in healthy ways. Fostering open communication ensures that no one feels isolated in their struggles. Safe spaces for honest conversations, feedback, and prayer must be normalized.

Offer strategies for stress management, such as breathing exercises, reflection spaces, mindfulness workshops, or prayer groups. Create rhythms of emotional renewal where employees can regroup, recharge, and re-engage without shame.

How Small Acts Create Massive Change

Don't despise the small beginnings (Zechariah 4:10). One conversation can change a department. One act of forgiveness can shift a team. One prayer can break business, financial, and generational strongholds. One new habit can create a legacy.

Offer a listening ear to a coworker struggling quietly. Start a small prayer group or encouragement circle at your office. Host a *"Gratitude Wall"* where employees can post notes of appreciation. Celebrate every act of reconciliation, forgiveness, and collaboration.

These small acts, done consistently and in love, multiply beyond what you could ever orchestrate in your own strength. They ripple into families, churches, communities, and even future generations.

Do not despise these small beginnings, for the Lord rejoices to see the work begin. — Zechariah 4:10, NLT

You Are a Restorer

The world does not need more critics. It needs more Restorers. It needs you. Workplaces are restored and moved forward not by those who criticize broken places, but by those who *do something* to heal them.

By those who choose love when bitterness would be easier. By those who model forgiveness when retaliation seems justified. By those who lead with integrity when compromise would be more convenient. By those who serve when selfishness seems safer.

You are one of them. You are the living, breathing beginning of a workplace restoration movement. And it starts right now, right where you are.

Reflection Question

- What is one small action I can take today to start healing my workplace culture?
- Who can I encourage, mentor, or support in my current role?
- What legacy of healing and restoration do I want to leave behind?

Workplace Healing Action Steps

- Write a **Workplace Restorer's Commitment**: a personal mission statement for how you will lead, serve, and restore in your current assignment. Begin each workday with a 60-second prayer: *"God, help me to be a healer, not a hurter, today."*

- Initiate one new act of healing in your workplace this month, even if it seems small.

Destiny Declarations

Speak these boldly in faith:

- *Through Christ, I am a Restorer of broken places and broken people.*
- *My workplace is my mission field, and I carry healing in my hands and heart.*
- *The world will change because I chose to heal what was broken and love where others quit.*

Workplace Restoration Toolkit (Appendix Reference)

In the Appendix, you'll find:

- *Workplace Restorer's Manifesto Template*
- *Small Acts of Restoration Challenge List*
- *Personal Healing Growth Tracker*

(See Appendix A: Workplace Restoration Toolkit for next steps.)

Prayer: Lord, Let the Restoration Begin With Me

Heavenly Father,

Thank You for placing me exactly where I am for such a time as this. I acknowledge that my workplace is not just where I earn a living; it is where You have sent me to make a difference. I surrender my title, timeline, fears, and frustrations to You, and I boldly ask: *Use me, Lord, as a Restorer.*

Help me to see with Heaven's eyes: not just tasks, but

people; not just meetings, but divine appointments. Let every word I speak carry healing. Let every step I take be guided by grace. Let every choice I make reflect the power of love, humility, and integrity.

God, I invite You to heal what has been broken in me so I may carry healing into every place I lead, serve, and show up. Tear down any pride, fear, or bitterness that may hinder Your work through me. Plant in me the seeds of compassion, courage, and consistency so that I may bloom even in dry places.

When I feel unseen, *remind me that **You** see.* When I grow weary, strengthen me with Your joy. When I fall short, lift me with Your mercy and set me back on mission.

Make me a spring whose waters never fail. Let restoration ripple out of me to my coworkers, team, leaders, and beyond. Let the culture shift because I chose to show up healed. Let my legacy be one of healing, wholeness, and unwavering faithfulness.

I declare today: I am a Restorer. Through Christ, I have the power to rebuild broken bridges, rewrite toxic narratives, and release hope in hopeless spaces. And it starts with me, right here, right now.

In Jesus' Name, Amen.

CONCLUSION
The Workplace Revival: A New Era of Healing, Unity, and Purpose

Congratulations, you've completed more than just a book, you've walked through a commissioning. You've dared to see what others ignore, feel what others suppress, and dream of what many call impossible.

This journey hasn't just given you insight; it has given you identity. You are no longer simply an employee, a manager, a founder, or a coworker. You are something far greater. *You are a Restorer.*

A builder of bridges where division once reigned. A healer of wounds others were too afraid to touch. A cultivator of trust in places where suspicion once thrived. A releaser of purpose in people who had forgotten they mattered. A lighthouse in the fog of workplace chaos and burnout. And the world is waiting, eagerly, for what you carry.

You were not randomly placed in your job. You were assigned. Not just to complete tasks, but to transform territory. To carry the atmosphere of Heaven into conference rooms, break rooms, Zoom calls, and Monday morning meetings.

To see cubicles and campuses not just as workplaces, but as Kingdom ground. To wake up each day with the quiet conviction: *"Healing begins with me."*

This is your era. This is your invitation. You were born and chosen for this. You were equipped for this.

So go. Lead with love. Speak with wisdom. Honor without compromise. Forgive freely. Set boundaries boldly. Model restoration daily. And never, ever forget who you are:

A Restorer.
An Atmosphere Shifter.
A Culture Builder.
A Destiny Unlocker.

The workplace transformation has begun. And it starts with you.

What You Have Learned

Throughout this book, you have gathered powerful tools, timeless wisdom, and Kingdom empowerment to walk boldly into your calling. You now have everything you need to:

- Heal broken relationships with grace and truth
- Build trust where betrayal once lived
- Communicate in ways that heal rather than harm
- Foster emotional intelligence, resilience, and unity
- Set boundaries that protect your energy and preserve your purpose
- Create cultures of belonging, honor, and radical hope
- Restore teams fractured by fear, ego, or disillusionment
- Lead with love, courage, humility, and unwavering integrity
- Design organizations that heal people and prosper ethically
- Unlock not only your destiny, but help others dis-

cover theirs too.

You have been entrusted with solutions for the greatest crises facing workplaces today: toxic communication, broken trust, burnout, high turnover, fear-driven cultures, and loss of purpose.

You now hold within you the power to reverse what was meant for destruction and to usher in healing that will echo for generations. You are the answer you have been praying for. You are equipped, empowered, and ready.

A New Vision for the Workplace

Can you imagine walking into a workplace where healing is not the exception, but the expectation? Where unity hums through every hallway and competition is replaced by collaboration? Where purpose is not lost under piles of computer or paperwork, but activated and celebrated daily? Where trust runs deep, communication flows freely, and people leave work energized, not exhausted? Beloved, this isn't a fantasy. This is a new reality you are called to create, and it starts with you.

How to Cultivate Healing, Unity, and Purpose at Work

You already have the blueprint in your hands:

1. Build supportive environments rooted in trust, transparency, and shared values.
2. Foster open communication that welcomes every voice, even the quiet ones.
3. Emphasize vision and mission in every conversation, every meeting, and every decision.
4. Implement practices that nurture belonging, inclu-

sion, and emotional safety.

5. Lead with authenticity, empathy, and courage, whether you hold a title or not.

Healing workplaces don't happen by accident. They happen because courageous people like you dare to dream bigger, love deeper, and lead differently. You won't just transform organizations through healing, unity, and purpose; you will restore lives, heal families, reignite communities, and leave legacies that echo in eternity.

The Author's Heart for You

As the author of this book, and even more, as your sister in Christ, your fellow Restorer, your empowerment coach, and your greatest encourager, I want you to know this with every fiber of your being:

- I believe in you.
- I love you with the love of Christ.
- And I am cheering for your victory every single day.

This book was not written from a place of theory or detached research. It was born from real-life battles, real prayers, real breakthroughs, being a wife for over 25 years, a mother of seven incredible children, and a life and empowerment coach to women and leaders who are desperate to win in business, careers, their homes and families, and every arena of life.

I have seen firsthand what broken workplaces and shattered homes can do to a person's heart. And I have witnessed, just as powerfully, what a healed workplace can unleash: resilience, destiny, freedom, and joy.

You deserve to thrive, your coworkers deserve to succeed, and your organization deserves to become profitable *and* a beacon of hope in a hurting, cynical world. And *you are essential* to that healing story. You carry the seeds of wisdom and revival inside you, which will bear fruit for generations to come.

Your Call to Action: The Movement Starts with You

The Workplace Restoration Movement is not something that can be outsourced to someone more experienced, more credentialed, or more famous. It starts with you. It begins the moment you decide to live differently: to lead by example with courageous compassion, communicate with intentional kindness, honor with bold consistency, and serve with a heart full of Kingdom purpose.

It begins when you declare: "I will be a Restorer, even when it's hard. I will build when others tear down. I will love when others walk away. I will heal when others choose to hurt."

And when you take your first courageous step, you will realize something beautiful: You are not alone. Across the globe, thousands, even millions, of others are rising just like you.

Imagine what would happen if every workplace in every city, in every nation, were filled with Restorers. Imagine the revival that would sweep across offices, homes, and communities, lighting fires of healing and destiny wherever God's people go. You are part of that awakening. You are carrying it right now. And you were born for such a time as this (Esther 4:14).

Who knows if perhaps you were made...for just such a time as this?
—— *Esther 4:14, NLT*

Final Blessing and Commission

Now, cherished Restorer, I bless you with this: May the Lord bless you and keep you. May He make His face shine upon you and be gracious to you. May He empower you to heal what is broken, to unify what is divided, and to breathe fresh life into every space you enter.

You are not simply going to work anymore. You are going to battle for healing, hope, and restoration. You will stand where others fall, love where others quit, and restore what others said was impossible. And through your hands, heart, and faithfulness, God will transform workplaces and the world.

Now go. Build. Heal. Lead. Your destiny awaits, and the movement has already begun.

Reflection Questions

1. What workplace or relationship can I begin restoring today, even with one small act of healing?
2. How can I encourage others around me to rise as Restorers, too?
3. What personal commitment will I make daily to cultivate healing, unity, and purpose?

Final Workplace Healing Action Step

Create your personal Workplace Restorer's Commitment: a heartfelt, Spirit-led declaration of how you will live out healing, unity, and purpose wherever God plants you.

Final Destiny Declarations

Speak these out loud with boldness and faith:

- *Through Christ, I am a Restorer of workplaces, hearts, and destinies.*
- *I carry healing, unity, and purpose wherever I go.*
- *The world will be changed because I said yes to my Kingdom assignment.*

Workplace Restoration Toolkit (Appendix Reminder)

Before you go, be sure to dive into the full Appendix, where you'll find:

- *Healing Organization Checklists*
- *Culture Transformation Templates*
- *Workplace Restoration Action Plans*

And so much more practical, Spirit-led support to help you continue your restoration journey. You are ready. You are equipped. You are anointed for such a time as this. Let the Workplace Restoration Transformation and Revival begin, and let it start with you.

Workplace Restorer's Commitment

A sacred declaration of healing, leadership, and legacy.

I, _____, declare today that I am a Workplace Restorer.

I believe healing is necessary and possible, honor has power, and unity is achievable. I commit to carrying the light of restoration into every environment I step into. I choose love over ego, courage over silence, and peace over passivity. I understand that transformation doesn't start with a policy; it begins with a person, and I am that person.

From this day forward, I will:

- Speak words that build, not break.
- Create space for safety, growth, and grace.
- Lead with empathy, integrity, and accountability.
- Forgive quickly, communicate clearly, and listen deeply.
- Celebrate others and champion purpose.
- Set boundaries that protect my peace and expand my influence.
- Use my influence to uplift the unseen and honor the overlooked.
- Take courageous steps, even when no one else does.

I am not waiting on someone else to change the culture. I am the culture-shifter. I am the bridge-builder. I am the Restorer.

This is my calling. This is my commitment. This is my legacy.

Signed: _____

Date: _____

FINAL WORD

Beloved Restorer, you didn't just finish a book. You ignited a movement within you and within every environment you enter.

You now carry the tools, wisdom, and anointing to bring healing, unity, and destiny to every workplace you touch. You have been equipped for such a time as this, not by accident but by divine appointment.

There will be days when the work feels hard, moments when restoration feels slow, and seasons when it feels easier to retreat than to rebuild.

But remember this: every act of healing matters, every word of encouragement, every bridge you mend, every broken place you touch with hope. It all matters. It is seen, and it is changing the world.

You don't have to be the loudest voice. You just have to be the most faithful. One workplace at a time. One relationship at a time. One destiny at a time.

You are not alone. Restorers are rising across the globe, each carrying the same fire you now carry. And together, we will see transformation sweep across workplaces, cities, and nations.

The future belongs to healers. You get one life to impact others and every environment you enter. The world is waiting. The Kingdom is advancing, and it all starts with one willing heart, yours. So go. Build. Heal. Lead. Love. Restore. Your destiny is calling, and Heaven is cheering you on. You were born for this.

Final Blessing

May the Lord bless you with abundant wisdom, uncommon favor, and divine courage as you step into your calling.

May your hands heal what was broken.

May your words breathe life into weary hearts.

May your leadership ignite hope where despair once ruled.

May your presence bring peace into every room you enter.

May you be like a well-watered garden; ever flourishing, ever fruitful, regardless of the conditions around you.

May every seed of healing you plant produce a harvest far beyond what you can imagine, touching generations you may never even see.

And may you walk daily in the joy, the strength, and the anointing of the One who called you: faithful, fearless, and forever victorious.

In Jesus' mighty Name, Amen.

WORKPLACE RESTORER'S COMMITMENT

Today, I make a sacred commitment. Before God, myself, and those I am called to impact, I choose to step boldly into my assignment as a Workplace Restorer.

I commit to:

1. Heal where others have wounded.
2. Build trust where betrayal once lived.
3. Communicate with compassion, not criticism.
4. Lead with love, courage, and integrity, even when it costs me.
5. Create spaces of belonging, honor, and safety wherever I go.
6. Encourage emotional health, resilience, and wholeness in myself and in others.
7. Champion diversity, dignity, wisdom, and Kingdom purpose in every environment.
8. Set healthy boundaries that protect my calling and my peace.
9. Pursue continuous growth with humility, passion, and perseverance.
10. Choose service over selfishness, unity over division, and hope over fear.

I declare that my workplace is not just a job site:

- It is my mission field.
- It is my training ground.
- It is my platform for Kingdom impact.

I will not wait for perfect conditions. I will not shrink back when challenges arise. I will sow healing seeds today, knowing that tomorrow's harvest depends on my faithfulness now.

I trust that God goes before me, strengthens me, and works through me to heal what has been broken, to unite what has been divided, and to unlock destinies yet unseen.

I am a Restorer.
I am a Builder of Bridges.
I am a Carrier of Healing, Unity, and Purpose.
And I say YES to my assignment, with all my heart.

Signed: _____

Date: _____

He who began a good work in you will be faithful to complete it.
— Philippians 1:6

Appendix A

Tools for Workplace Transformation

Chapter 1: The Silent Epidemic: Broken Relationships in the Modern Workplace

1. Sample Dialogue for Healing Miscommunication

Purpose: Use this template when communication between team members or departments has broken down. It models humility, clarity, and active listening.

Scenario Example: A manager misinterprets a team member's email tone and responds harshly in front of others.

Restorative Dialogue Script:

Manager: "Hi [Name], I want to take a moment to acknowledge how I responded in our last meeting. I realize I misread your email and responded too quickly. I regret that and apologize for reacting without seeking clarity first."

Team Member: "Thank you for saying that. I was surprised during the meeting and felt misunderstood. I didn't intend for the email to sound dismissive."

Manager: "I appreciate you clarifying that. In the future, let's agree to pause and check in if something feels off, rather than assuming intent."

Team Member: "That sounds good. I value our ability to communicate openly and move forward."

Empowerment Strategy:

- Practice "Pause and Clarify" before reacting.
- Assume positive intent.
- Use the words "Help me understand..." to invite safe discussion.

2. Trust-Building Activity for Teams

Activity Name: "The Trust Wall"

Purpose: Strengthen team trust by acknowledging the unseen strengths and unseen burdens teammates carry.

Time Needed: 45 minutes

Materials: Sticky notes, markers, blank wall, or whiteboard

Instructions:

Give each person a stack of sticky notes in two colors.
On Color A, they write strengths they believe they bring to the team (one per note).
On Color B, they anonymously write things they often carry silently at work (e.g., fear of failure, workload stress).
One by one, they add both types of notes to the "Trust

Wall."

Once posted, the team leader guides a conversation:

- What surprised you?

- What do we need more empathy for?

- How can we better support one another moving forward?

Empowerment Strategy:

- Create a quarterly rhythm of emotional check-ins.
- Follow up with buddy partnerships or empathy training.

3. Guide for Conflict Resolution Conversations

Purpose: Offer a framework to approach conflict with humility and a solution-focused approach.

Step-by-Step Guide:

Step 1: Prepare Your Heart
Pray or reflect before speaking. Release assumptions or the need to "win."

Step 2: Choose the Right Time and Setting
Schedule a private, quiet space where both parties can feel safe.

Step 3: Use "I" Statements to Express Feelings
Example: "I felt overlooked when the decision was made without my input."

Step 4: Seek to Understand

Ask, "Can you help me understand your perspective on what happened?" Listen actively and reflect what you hear: "So what I hear you saying is..."

Step 5: Clarify Intentions and Impact

Discuss how actions were interpreted versus intended. Express a shared desire to move forward.

Step 6: Co-Create a Path Forward

Ask: "What can we do differently next time?" Agree on communication or behavior shifts.

Empowerment Strategy: Use a "Conflict Journal" to reflect before and after tough conversations. Train your team on this method through role-play workshops.

4. Prayer Prompts for Workplace Restoration

Use these prayers as daily or weekly prompts to invite God into your workplace healing process.

Prayer for Unity:

"Lord, make us one in heart and spirit. Help us lay aside ego, offense, and division. Let our differences be strengths, not stumbling blocks.

Prayer for Clarity:

"Holy Spirit, guide our conversations. Give us words that bring peace, not pain. Show us how to speak the truth in love."

Prayer for Leadership:

"Father, give me wisdom and humility to lead with integrity. Help me model what I want to see in others."

Prayer for the Wounded:
"God, you see every heart carrying hidden pain. Heal what is broken. Comfort those grieving, frustrated, or burnt out."

Prayer of Commission:
"I receive my assignment to be a Restorer. Use me to be a voice of peace, a vessel of healing, and a light in dark places. Amen."

Empowerment Tip: Use these prompts in meetings, personal devotionals, or group reflections. Pair each with a 60-second reflection or journaling moment for more profound impact. These tools are designed to move your message from inspiration into implementation. *Transformation begins when wisdom becomes action.*

CHAPTER 2: BEYOND PROFIT: THE HUMAN COST OF A BROKEN WORK CULTURE

Sample Employee Engagement Survey

Use this sample survey to assess the current level of employee engagement in your workplace. Keep it anonymous to promote honest feedback. Responses will help guide leadership decisions and spark meaningful culture improvements.

Instructions: Rate each statement from 1 (Strongly Disagree) to 5 (Strongly Agree)

___I feel valued and appreciated by my team.

___I understand how my work contributes to the mission of this organization.

___I have the tools and support I need to do my job well.

___I feel safe giving honest feedback to my supervisor or leadership.

___My ideas and suggestions are welcome and considered.

___I receive recognition when I do good work.

___I trust the leadership team.

___I have opportunities to grow personally and professionally.

___I feel a sense of belonging here.

___Overall, I am satisfied with my job.

Quick Guide: How to Encourage a Discouraged Team Member

When a team member seems withdrawn, disengaged, or disheartened, a few intentional moments of care can reignite their confidence and purpose.

Step 1: Notice and Initiate: Approach the person privately with humility and care. Example: "I've noticed you haven't seemed like yourself lately, and I just wanted to check in."

Step 2: Listen Without Fixing: Let them speak without rushing to give advice. Ask, "What's been weighing on you lately?" or "What would feel supportive right now?"

Step 3: Affirm Their Strengths: Share a specific affirmation. Example: "You bring so much creativity and steadiness to this team. Your presence matters."

Step 4: Offer Tangible Support: Ask how you can help. Suggest a break, adjusting workload, or just walking with them through a hard day. Even small gestures create safety.

Step 5: Follow Up: Encouragement should be ongoing. A quick message, a handwritten note, or a follow-up coffee chat keeps the relationship nurtured.

Checklist for Building a Culture of Honor

A culture of honor starts with intentional action. Use this checklist with your leadership team, HR department, or small group to track progress.

- Leadership & Recognition
- Communication
- Inclusivity & Belonging
- Policies & Practice

Pro-Tip: Add one "Honor Highlight" to every team meeting, where someone is celebrated not just for what they do, but for who they are.

CHAPTER 3: TRUST, SAFETY, PURPOSE: THE REAL BOTTOM LINE

Trust-Building Exercises for Teams

Purpose: Strengthen communication, increase trust, and deepen collaboration through interactive group activities.

1. The Values Wall

Objective: Align the team around shared values.

How to Do It: Write 10–15 workplace values (e.g., respect, honesty, empathy, creativity, responsibility) on large sticky notes or a whiteboard.

Ask each team member to vote for their top 3. Tally the votes and have a group discussion:

- Why are these values important to us?
- How can we live them out daily?

Bonus: Turn the top values into a visible "Team Code of Honor" posted in the office or digital workspace.

2. The Trust Circle

Objective: Build psychological safety and vulnerability

How to Do It: Sit in a circle. Each person completes the prompt:

- "One thing I appreciate about this team is…"
- "One thing I'd love to see us grow in is…"

Rules:

- No interruptions, corrections, or debate.
- Everyone listens with openness.
- The facilitator ends with a short encouragement, prayer, or moment of gratitude.

3. "If I Were You..." Empathy Exercise

Objective: Strengthen empathy and reduce judgment.

How to Do It: Divide into pairs. One person shares a recent work challenge.

The other responds with:

- "If I were in your shoes, I'd probably feel ___."
- "What I might need in that moment is ___."

Switch roles and debrief as a group about what they learned through listening instead of solving.

Sample Feedback Invitation Templates

Purpose: Normalize feedback as a path to growth, not fear. These templates help you invite feedback with clarity, humility, and professionalism.

Template 1: Peer-to-Peer

Subject: I'd Love Your Honest Feedback

Hi [Name],
I'm committed to growing in how I support the team, and I value your perspective. Would you be willing to share:
- One thing I'm doing well
- One area I could improve

Feel free to share by email or in a quick chat. I appreciate your honesty and insight.
Gratefully,
[Your Name]

Template 2: Manager to Team

Subject: Help Me Lead You Better

Team,

I want to continue growing as a leader, and your feedback helps me serve you more clearly and with care. Would you anonymously share:

- What helps you feel most supported by me?
- What do you need more of (or less of) from me as your leader?

I've created a short feedback form here: [Insert Link]
Thank you for helping me grow.

Template 3: Team to New Hire

Subject: Welcome, And We'd Love to Hear from You!

Hi [New Hire's Name],

As you settle in, we'd love to hear your first impressions. Your fresh perspective is so valuable.

- What's been working well so far?
- Is there anything confusing or unclear?
- How can we better support you this week?

You're an essential part of this team already. Let us know how we can help you thrive.

Psychological Safety Assessment Worksheet

Purpose: A quick team or self-assessment to measure

and strengthen the level of psychological safety in your work environment.

Instructions: Rate each statement on a scale of 1–5
(1 = Strongly Disagree | 5 = Strongly Agree)

Communication & Voice

____I feel safe expressing my thoughts without fear of embarrassment.

____I can offer a dissenting opinion without being punished or excluded.

____Leaders regularly invite honest feedback and act on it.

Relationships & Respect

____Team members treat each other with dignity and professionalism.

____I've seen people admit mistakes without judgment.

____Healthy conflict is resolved openly and respectfully.

Trust & Transparency

____I trust leadership to follow through on their word.

____When mistakes are made, they are addressed fairly, not with blame.

____I feel empowered to speak up about risks, ideas, or problems.

Growth & Safety

____I can take reasonable risks without fear of retaliation.

___Learning and vulnerability are encouraged, not punished.

Feedback is used as a tool for growth, not shame.

Scoring Guide:

Add up your total score and use the guide below:
45–60: Strong Psychological Safety
30–44: Moderate: Great opportunity to improve
Below 30: Low: Prioritize culture healing strategies

CHAPTER 4: EMOTIONAL INTELLIGENCE: THE CORE SKILL OF THE RESTORED WORKPLACE

Emotional Intelligence Self-Assessment

Purpose: To help individuals assess their current emotional intelligence (EQ) level and identify areas of strength and growth. EQ is foundational for communication, conflict resolution, leadership, and team success.

Instructions: Rate yourself on a scale of 1–5 for each statement below:
(1 = Strongly Disagree | 5 = Strongly Agree)

Self-Awareness

___I recognize when I am emotionally triggered.
___I can identify what I'm feeling without blaming others.
___I understand how my emotions impact my decisions and actions.

Self-Management

____I can remain calm under pressure.

____I can pause and respond wisely instead of reacting impulsively.

____I manage stress in healthy, constructive ways.

Social Awareness

____I can sense when someone else is upset, even if they don't say it.

____I seek to understand people's perspectives before offering mine.

____I notice how team dynamics affect others emotionally.

Relationship Management

____I handle difficult conversations with honesty and care.

____I apologize when I've hurt someone and seek reconciliation.

____I strive to build trust and connection with the people I work with.

Scoring

45–60: Strong EQ: You are a Restorer-in-action. Keep building!

30–44: Developing EQ: Great awareness, with growth opportunities.

Below 30: EQ Awakening: This is your moment to begin the transformation.

Next Step: Highlight your lowest-scoring statements

and journal through what might be driving that challenge. Set one micro-goal per area to improve your emotional intelligence over the next 30 days.

Sample Active Listening Exercise for Teams

Purpose: To increase empathy, reduce misunderstandings, and help teams practice attentive, non-defensive listening.

Time Required: 15–20 minutes

How to Facilitate: Pair Up Team Members. One is the Speaker, the other is the Listener

Speaker Prompt (Choose One):

- "One thing I'm excited about in our work is…"
- "One thing that's been challenging for me lately is…"
- "Something I wish people better understood about me is…"

The Listener's Role: Maintain eye contact. Do not interrupt or advise. Nod or acknowledge only with short affirmations ("I hear you," "Thanks for sharing").

After 2–3 minutes, mirror what you heard by saying:

- "What I hear you saying is…"
- "It sounds like you feel…"
- "Is that right?"

Then wait for confirmation or clarification. Switch roles

and repeat the process.

Debrief as a Group: Ask:

1. How did it feel to be truly listened to?
2. What surprised you about your partner's experience?
3. How might this kind of listening improve our culture?

Bonus Tip: Use this at the start of team meetings for a 5-minute check-in.

Emotional Triggers Journal Template

Purpose: To help individuals recognize emotional triggers, break unhealthy response patterns, and build self-awareness that leads to wiser communication and relationships.

Instructions: Use this template anytime you feel emotionally activated at work (e.g., frustrated, angry, anxious, shut down, defensive).

Trigger Reflection Prompt

1. What Happened?
(Briefly describe the situation.)
Example: "My idea was dismissed in a meeting."

2. What Did I Feel?
(Check all that apply or add your own.)

☐ Frustrated

- ☐ Disrespected
- ☐ Embarrassed
- ☐ Overlooked
- ☐ Triggered by tone
- ☐ Angry
- ☐ Defensive
- ☐ Insecure
- ☐ _____
- ☐ _____

3. What Did I Think?
(Write the internal thoughts you had.)
- "They don't value me."
- "This always happens."
- "I'll just keep quiet next time."

4. What Was the Root Cause?
(Was this about the moment, or something deeper?)
- Fear of being rejected
- Feeling unheard in the past
- Pressure to prove myself
- A need for affirmation
- Old wound being reopened

5. What Could I Do Differently Next Time?
(Write a healthier response for next time.)
- "Pause and breathe before reacting."
- "Ask for clarity without assuming."
- "Follow up after the meeting to share my idea calmly."

6. What Do I Need to Heal from This?
- Forgiveness
- Encouragement

- Clarity
- Feedback
- Boundaries
- Prayer

7. Prayer Prompt (Optional):

"Lord, help me to respond with wisdom, not emotion. Heal the root of this reaction and help me speak with clarity and compassion."

Chapter 5: Building and Rebuilding Trust

Sample Trust- Building Plan Template

Purpose: To provide leaders and teams with a clear, pro-active strategy for rebuilding or reinforcing trust after it has been broken or neglected.

When to Use:
- After conflict, turnover, restructuring, or communication breakdowns
- When onboarding new leadership or teams
- During a culture reset initiative

Trust-Building Plan: 30-Day Blueprint

1. Identify the Trust Gap

Ask:

- What behaviors or events caused trust to weaken?
- What is currently missing in team dynamics?

Example: "Lack of follow-through on deadlines has led to resentment."

2. Establish Shared Language for Trust

As a team, define what trust looks like in your workplace.

Use prompts like:

- "Trust means _____."
- "I feel most trusted when _____."
- "A trustworthy team does _____."

3. Clarify Commitments & Expectations

Reinforce the importance of reliability and role clarity.

Action Items:

- Clarify job roles and key responsibilities
- Confirm timelines, deadlines, and follow-ups
- Reaffirm what can be expected of leadership and team members.

4. Initiate Weekly Trust Touchpoints

Build a connection through consistent communication.

Ideas:

- Monday 15-minute stand-up huddles
- Weekly 1:1s between managers and team members
- Friday "Wins + Where We're Growing" check-ins

5. Celebrate Trust in Action

Catch people doing the right thing. Publicly affirm actions that rebuild trust (follow-through, owning mistakes, kindness under pressure).

Example Script: "I want to recognize Alex for honoring their word on that tough deadline. That's how we build trust around here."

6. Review + Reflect at 30 Days

Host a team check-in to discuss:

- What's working?
- What still needs healing?
- What should we continue or shift?

Steps to an Effective Workplace Apology

Purpose: To help team members restore relational trust after miscommunication, mistakes, or conflict.

Remember: An apology is not weakness; it's wisdom in action. It's how leaders and teammates build bridges, not walls.

The 5-Step Framework for a Transformational Apology

1. Acknowledge the Specific Impact

Say exactly what happened and how it affected the other person.

"I realize my comment during the meeting made you

feel dismissed, and I'm truly sorry for that."

Don't say: "If I offended you..." (That minimizes their experience.)

2. Take Ownership, Without Excuses

Avoid defensiveness. This is about responsibility, not justification
Say: "That was on me. I should've slowed down and listened."

Don't say: "Well, I was stressed, and you caught me at a bad time..."

3. Express Sincere Regret

Let them feel your heart.
"I value our working relationship and hate that I caused harm."

4. Ask for Forgiveness (If Appropriate)

You're not demanding it, you're honoring their process.

"I hope you can forgive me, and I want to make this right."

5. Clarify Your Plan for Change

This is the most critical piece. Apologies without action are empty.

Say: "Moving forward, I'll pause before responding and

commit to following up with you directly."

Say: "I've set a reminder to check in weekly so we don't fall out of sync."

Checklist for Transparent Communication Practices

Purpose: To help individuals and teams build a culture where communication is honest, consistent, and kind, the bedrock of high-trust environments.

Transparency Checklist for Leaders and Teams

Communication Culture
☐ We communicate early, not just when issues explode.
☐ We give feedback in real-time, not just during reviews.
☐ We are clear on how we communicate (email, chat, meetings).

Leadership Modeling
☐ Leaders admit when they don't know or make a mistake.
☐ Leadership decisions are explained with the "why," not just the "what."
☐ Bad news is shared with empathy, not hidden or sugar-coated.

Meeting Clarity
☐ Agendas are provided ahead of time.
☐ Everyone knows their role in the meeting (lead, contribute, observe).
☐ Outcomes and next steps are documented and re-

capped clearly.

Feedback Practices
☐ Feedback is expected, welcomed, and normalized.
☐ We use "feed-forward" language, focused on future growth.
☐ There are clear, safe channels for anonymous concerns.

Team Communication Norms
☐ We avoid gossip and triangulation, we talk to people, not about them.
☐ We assume positive intent but clarify when needed.
☐ We use "I" language when sharing a challenge:

- Say: "*I* felt overwhelmed during that change…"
- Don't say: "You guys always change things last-minute!"

Crisis or Conflict
☐ We inform affected people early.
☐ We over-communicate during uncertainty.
☐ We offer compassion, clarity, and connection, not just control.

CHAPTER 6: COMMUNICATION THAT HEALS INSTEAD OF HURTS

Healing Conversation Starters for Teams

Purpose: To spark meaningful, trust-building conversations that foster connection, empathy, and a culture of restoration. These prompts are perfect for team meetings, retreats, one-on-ones, or conflict recovery moments.

When to Use:
- Team check-ins or huddles
- Conflict resolution debriefs
- Staff development days
- Employee support conversations

Team Connection Prompts:
1. "What's one thing that helps you feel valued at work?" *Why it works:* Reveals emotional drivers for motivation and belonging.
2. "What's one strength you admire in someone on this team?" *Why it works:* Builds a culture of encouragement and recognition
3. "What helps you feel safe to share ideas or concerns here?" *Why it works:* Promotes psychological safety and feedback transparency.
4. "When was a time you felt especially supported at work?" *Why it works:* Surfaces healthy behaviors to reinforce.
5. "What's one thing you wish people better understood about you?" *Why it works:* Encourages empathy and dismantles assumptions
6. "How do you prefer to receive feedback, in the moment or privately?" *Why it works:* It builds respect around communication styles.
7. "What's something small we could do as a team to bring more joy to our workdays?" *Why it works:* Invites creativity, ownership, and shared morale

Empowerment Tip: Rotate one question per meeting and give everyone 30–60 seconds to respond. Keep it light, safe, and voluntary, there should be no pressure to share.

Self-Assessment: How Healing Are My Words?

Purpose: To reflect on the impact of your daily communication style and identify areas for healing, growth, and intentionality.

Instructions: Answer honestly. There are no right or wrong answers, only insight. Use this as a personal check-in or team discussion tool.

Reflective Questions (Rate Yourself 1–5)
Question   1 = Rarely   5 = Always

___I speak kindly even under pressure.

___I pause and think before responding emotionally.

___I give feedback that uplifts, not just critiques.

___I listen fully before forming my response.

___I avoid sarcasm, gossip, or passive-aggressive comments.

___I seek to understand before I seek to be understood.

___I speak life, not just logic.

Reflection Prompts

1. What is one thing I can start saying more often to build others up?
2. Where have I noticed my words causing unintended harm?
3. Who might need an encouraging message from me today?

Coaching Cue: Share your reflections in a journal or with a trusted mentor. Growth begins with awareness.

Script Templates for Giving and Receiving Feedback with Grace

Purpose: To equip leaders and team members with clear, empowering words that turn feedback into a healing, collaborative experience, not a dreaded conversation.

Script 1: Giving Constructive Feedback

Opening with care:
"Hey [Name], I appreciate the value you bring to our team and the effort I see you putting in…"

Share the observation (not judgment):
"I noticed during yesterday's presentation that a few deadlines were missed, and it caused some confusion for the client."

Express impact, not accusation:
"This impacted our ability to follow through, and I want to ensure we're aligned going forward."

Invite growth collaboratively:
"Can we walk through what might've caused the delay and how we can support each other better next time?"

Close with belief and encouragement:
"I believe in your potential, and I know this is something we can improve together."

Script 2: Receiving Feedback Gracefully

Acknowledge and disarm:
"Thank you for bringing that to my attention. I really

appreciate your honesty."

Clarify, don't defend:
"Can you help me understand more about how that came across?"

Own your part:
"I can see how that impacted the team. That wasn't my intention, but I take responsibility for how it landed.

Commit to growth:
"Moving forward, I'll be more mindful of [specific behavior]. Thanks again for the feedback."

Empowerment Reminder: Feedback is a gift. Receiving it well is a superpower that builds emotional maturity, influence, and trust.

Chapter 7: Psychological Safety: The New Superpower of Organizations

Psychological Safety Assessment Survey

Purpose: To help teams and leaders identify strengths and gaps in *psychological safety,* the #1 predictor of high-performing teams.

Instructions:
Invite each team member to rate the following statements anonymously on a scale of 1–5. (1 = Strongly Disagree, 5 = Strongly Agree)

Statement Rating (1–5)

____I feel safe to speak up with ideas, questions, or concerns.

____I can admit mistakes or weaknesses without fear of embarrassment.

____I feel that my contributions are valued and taken seriously.

____I feel respected by my peers and leaders.

____Feedback (both positive and constructive) is shared openly here.

____I see leaders model vulnerability and humility.

____When conflict arises, it is addressed respectfully and not avoided.

____I am encouraged to try new things, even if mistakes might occur.

____Diverse perspectives are welcomed, not shut down.

____I trust my team to support me, even in high-stress moments.

Scoring & Reflection:

41–50: Healthy psychological safety, keep growing!

31–40: Stable, but room to deepen team trust and communication.

Below 30: Prioritize safety-building practices immediately (see tips below).

Next Steps:

- Share anonymous team results.
- Host a "Let's Grow Together" session to identify two commitments the team can make.
- Consider follow-up coaching or a professional team-building session.
- Sample Scripts for Encouraging Courageous Conversations

- Use these gentle but direct scripts to open meaningful dialogue in challenging workplace situations.

Script 1: Addressing Tension Between Teammates

"I've noticed there may be some tension between us. I value working with you, and I'd love to understand what I can do differently to support a better connection moving forward."

Script 2: Inviting Honest Feedback from a Colleague

"I trust your insight, and I want to grow. Would you be willing to share one thing I could do to be a better teammate?"

Script 3: Offering Constructive Feedback with Grace

"Can I share something I've noticed that I believe could help us both thrive? I'm saying this because I believe in your value here."

Script 4: Starting a Hard Conversation with a Leader

"I respect you, and this may be a little uncomfortable, but I believe it's important for trust and growth. Can we talk about something I've been carrying?"

Tip: Always follow up courageous conversations with affirmation and listening. Ask:

- "What do you need from me now?" or
- "Is there anything I can do to support healing or progress?"

Checklist for Creating a Belonging Culture

Use this as a team or leadership reflection guide to assess and strengthen your workplace culture.

☐ We actively invite input and feedback from all team members.

☐ Our team reflects diversity in background, experience, and perspectives.

☐ Everyone knows they matter, not just for what they do, but for who they are.

☐ Recognition and celebrations are inclusive and personalized.

☐ We have mentorship or coaching pathways available to all.

☐ We normalize rest, recovery, and wellness.

☐ New employees are welcomed with intentional connection.

☐ We regularly talk about values like kindness, collaboration, and respect.

☐ People feel emotionally safe to express disagreement or concern.

☐ Stories of belonging, reconciliation, and courage are shared openly.

Action Step

Choose three that are not consistently true yet. For each one, ask:

1. "What would it look like to bring this to life here?"
2. "What barrier do we need to remove to make this happen?

Bonus Empowerment Tip: If you want to make these resources even more meaningful, invite your team to complete them together at a team retreat or staff meeting, turning each tool into a catalyst for culture transformation.

Chapter 8: Healing the Heart You Bring to Work

Personal Heart-Check Reflection Worksheet

Use this reflection to identify emotional warning signs and reset your heart before the next workweek.

Instructions: Take 10 minutes in a quiet space. Reflect and journal honestly. Use this worksheet weekly to track your growth.

1. How am I really feeling about work this week?
(Use words like: hopeful, anxious, frustrated, grateful, numb, energized.)
2. What moment (or conversation) impacted me the most emotionally this week? Why?
3. Did I bring any unprocessed hurt, fear, or stress into my workplace relationships this week?
4. Did I communicate clearly and kindly this week, or did I avoid, react, or withdraw?
5. What do I need to release to God so I can return to work with peace and purpose?
6. What truth or Scripture can anchor me moving for-

ward?

(*Example:* "Create in me a clean heart, O God, and renew a right and steadfast spirit within me." – Psalm 51:10, AMP).

Boundary-Setting Scripts for Difficult Conversations

Use these graceful yet firm templates when you need to set boundaries that protect your time, peace, and energy.

Scenario 1: Someone repeatedly interrupts your breaks or after-hours time

Script:

"I care deeply about our team and want to give my best during work hours. To protect that, I've committed to not answering messages after 6 PM so I can rest and reset. I'll be happy to revisit this first thing tomorrow morning."

Scenario 2: You're being asked to take on too much without support

Script:

"I'd love to contribute to this, but I want to honor my existing priorities so I can deliver with excellence. Can we discuss shifting timelines or reallocating tasks so nothing gets dropped?"

Scenario 3: You need emotional space from a draining team dynamic

Script:

"I value our working relationship, and I've realized I need to create a little more space around emotionally charged topics so I can stay grounded and focused. I'm happy to collaborate, just from a healthier distance right now."

Faith-Based Softener (Add to any script if appropriate)

"I've been praying about how to lead from a place of peace, not pressure. I'm learning to honor what God's teaching me about balance, and this is one way I'm practicing that."

Self-Care and Healing Routine Planner

Authentic workplace restoration starts with daily soul restoration. Use this weekly planner to schedule healing into your life, not just your to-do list.

Monday
Morning Reset: Prayer + Gratitude journaling
Midday Grounding: 5-minute breathwork + walk
Evening Wind-Down: Screen-free dinner + worship music
Bonus Care: Encouragement text to a teammate

Tuesday
Morning Reset: Read 1 Scripture + affirmation
Midday Grounding: Drink water + stretch
Evening Wind-Down: Reflect on one workplace win
Bonus Care: Listen to a faith-based podcast

Wednesday
Morning Reset: Light exercise + declaration
Midday Grounding: Pause for three deep breaths before meetings

Evening Wind-Down: Phone-free prayer walk
Bonus Care: Leave work on time, no matter what

Thursday

Morning Reset: Speak a declaration aloud: "I bring peace, not pressure."

Midday Grounding: Sit in sunlight for 10 min

Evening Wind-Down: Journal 3 things I'm grateful for

Bonus Care: Watch or read something uplifting and funny

Friday

Morning Reset: Read Psalm 23 slowly

Midday Grounding: Say "no" to unnecessary requests

Evening Wind-Down: Celebrate a team member or yourself

Bonus Care: Sabbath prep: Plan rest this weekend

CHAPTER 9: FORGIVENESS: THE LEADERSHIP ADVANTAGE NOBODY TALKS ABOUT

Forgiveness Reflection Journal Prompts

Use this guided journaling session to release emotional burdens and experience freedom through forgiveness, personally and professionally.

Be kind and helpful to one another, tender-hearted {compassionate, understanding}, forgiving one another {readily and freely}, just as God in Christ also forgave you. — Ephesians 4:32, AMP

Instructions: Journal honestly. There are no wrong answers. These prompts are meant to uncover unresolved issues so God can heal them.

1. Who or what still stirs frustration, sadness, or bitterness in me when I think about work?

2. What do I feel I lost in this situation (trust, time, dignity, voice, opportunity)? How has that loss shaped the way I show up today?

3. Have I ever made assumptions that may have deepened the conflict?

4. What would I say if I could express myself fully, without fear of judgment or retaliation?

5. What does forgiveness look like in this situation? (Does it mean releasing, apologizing, drawing boundaries, or inviting healing?)

6. What Scripture can guide my heart toward peace?

7. What truth do I want to declare moving forward?

"I release _____ and receive peace (& wiser use of my time) in its place."

Sample Scripts for Conflict Resolution Conversations

Use these grace-filled templates to resolve workplace conflict with clarity, empathy, and courage.

If your brother or sister sins, go and point out their fault, just between the two of you. If they listen to you, you have won them over.
— *Matthew 18:15, NIV.*

If You Need to Start a Healing Conversation:

Script:

"I've been reflecting and praying, and I'd love to talk with you about something that's been on my heart. I value our relationship and believe we can grow stronger through honest, respectful dialogue."

If You Felt Disrespected or Misunderstood:

Script:

"Something happened that I'd like to clear the air on. I felt [hurt/confused/disrespected] when [describe behavior], and I just want to understand what was happening for you, too. I'm open to hearing your perspective.

If You Need to Apologize or Take Ownership:

Script:

"I've been thinking about our last interaction and want to own my part. I realize I [name the action or behavior] and can see how that may have impacted you. I'm truly sorry, and I want to make it right."

If You Want to Rebuild Trust:

Script:

"I know we've been distant, and I'd love to rebuild trust. Would you be open to meeting weekly or checking in more often so we can communicate better moving forward?"

Grace Note Add-On (Optional):

"I'm praying for wisdom and healing in this conversation, and I appreciate your willingness to meet me here."

Prayer Guide for Forgiveness and Workplace Restoration

Invite God into the healing process. Pray these daily, or when conflict arises.

Prayer for a Softened Heart

"Lord, remove the hardness from my heart. I don't want to carry bitterness into my workday. Give me compassion where I've felt hurt, and humility where I've caused harm. Create in me a clean heart, O God."

Prayer Before a Difficult Conversation

"Father, go before me. Prepare their heart and mine. Let this conversation be seasoned with grace. Help me speak truth in love, listen without defensiveness, and lead with the goal of peace, not pride."

Prayer for Releasing Offense

"God, I release the burden of this offense to You. I'm tired of carrying what You've already overcome. I forgive, not because they deserve it, but because I refuse to stay bound. I trust You to handle what I cannot."

Prayer to Be a Restorer at Work

"Jesus, make me a Restorer in my workplace. Use my words to heal, my presence to bring peace, and my leadership to reflect Your love. Let reconciliation be part of my legacy wherever I work or lead."

CHAPTER 10: BOUNDARIES THAT HEAL, NOT HARDEN

Boundary Setting Worksheet for Professionals

Healthy boundaries aren't selfish; they are a form of professional stewardship.

Above all else, guard your heart, for everything you do flows from it. – Proverbs 4:23 NIV

Use this worksheet to clarify, communicate, and reinforce personal and professional boundaries that protect your well-being, maximize your purpose, and sustain your calling.

STEP 1: Clarify Your Boundaries

What drains you most during your workweek?
- ☐ Excessive meetings
- ☐ Constant interruptions
- ☐ After-hours emails or calls
- ☐ Unrealistic deadlines
- ☐ Emotional weight of team conflict
- ☐ Lack of alone time
- ☐ Other: _____

What restores your energy?
- ☐ Quiet time with God
- ☐ Focused work blocks
- ☐ Scheduled breaks or movement
- ☐ Encouraging team check-ins
- ☐ Turning off notifications
- ☐ Other: _____

STEP 2: Define Key Boundaries

Area: Time
Current Challenge: Late-night messages drain me
New Boundary: No work emails after 6 PM
First Step to Communicate It: Update calendar settings and team norms

Area: Focus
Current Challenge: Too many unscheduled check-ins
New Boundary: Set "Do Not Disturb" hours
First Step to Communicate It: Inform the team during the morning huddle

Area: Emotional
Current Challenge: Taking on everyone's stress
New Boundary: "I can support, but I can't fix it."
First Step to Communicate It: Script a supportive but firm response

STEP 3: Write Your Boundary Declaration

"To serve well and stay whole, I commit to setting and honoring boundaries around my _____ (time, energy, values, focus). These boundaries protect my peace, steward my calling, and support sustainable excellence."

Sample Scripts for Respectful Boundary Conversations

Say no with grace. Speak the truth with love. Stay rooted in peace.

When You Need to Say No (Without Guilt):
• "I want to give this my full attention, but I'm cur-

rently at capacity. Can we revisit this at a better time?"

- "I'm honored you asked, but I have to decline so I can honor other commitments I've already made."

When You Need to Reinforce Working Hours:
- "To give my best during working hours, I don't respond to emails after 6 PM, I'll follow up in the morning."
- "I'm working hard on protecting my evenings to rest and reset. I'll catch up with everything first thing tomorrow."

When Someone Crosses an Emotional Boundary:
- "I care deeply, and I want to support you. But I'm realizing this may be outside my lane. Have you considered talking to [HR, mentor, counselor]?"
- "I'm here for you, but I also want to be honest about what I can and can't hold right now. Can we find a healthy solution together for both of us?"

When You're Constantly Interrupted or Overbooked:
- "I'd love to give you my full attention. Would you mind scheduling time so I can prepare well and not rush our conversation?
- "Let's protect this project by keeping a consistent meeting rhythm. That way we're not scrambling last-minute or pulling focus mid-day."

Grace Note:

Boundaries don't push people away, they create a sustainable connection.

Technology Detox Guide for Work-Life Balance

Reclaim your time. Renew your mind. Refocus your mission.

Be still and know (recognize, understand) that I am God.
– Psalm 46:10, AMP.

Why Digital Detoxing Matters

Constant notifications, endless email pings, and blurred work/home lines lead to:

- Decreased focus
- Increased stress and anxiety
- Decision fatigue
- Emotional burnout
- Strained relationships

Healing your workplace starts by healing your habits and decreasing your screen time

Detox Strategies You Can Start Today

1. Set Tech-Free Time Blocks
Designate at least one hour per day and one whole evening per week where screens are OFF. Use this time to rest, reflect, pray, read, or reconnect with loved ones.

2. Turn Off Notifications
Silence non-essential app alerts on your phone and laptop. Keep only calls and urgent messages active during deep work or family time.

3. Set a "Last Screen Time" Hour

Choose a cutoff time for emails, texts, and scrolling (ex., 8:30 PM). Replace it with a wind-down routine like prayer, stretching, or journaling.

4. Use a Sabbath Tech Rest

Practice a digital sabbath once a week, 24 hours without social media, news, or work apps. Let your spirit detox, refocus, and breathe.

5. Create a Tech-Free Zone

Establish spaces (bedroom, dinner table, car rides) where devices are not allowed. Protect peace in places that matter most.

What to Do Instead of Scrolling:

- Journal: *"What am I feeling right now?"*
- Go for a walk and pray aloud
- Read a book that nourishes your spirit
- Write one hand-written thank-you card
- Rest without guilt
- Dream again

Reflection Prompt:

"When I protect my time and peace, I show God I trust Him to multiply my efforts."

CHAPTER 11: REPAIRING BROKEN BRIDGES AT WORK

Healing Conversation Templates

Use when miscommunication, conflict, or emotional

tension needs resolution in a team.

Purpose: These templates help initiate courageous conversations that de-escalate tension, promote understanding, and lead to mutual healing.

Template 1: The "I Value This Relationship" Starter

Use when you want to preserve the relationship and clarify misunderstandings.

"Hey {Name}, I've been reflecting on something that happened between us, and I realize it's important for me to share it. I value our relationship and want to ensure we're on the same page. Would you be open to chatting briefly about it?"

Template 2: The "Impact Without Blame" Opener

Use when someone's action has hurt you, but you want to communicate without accusation.

"I want to share something that's been weighing on me. When [describe the situation], I felt [describe emotion]. I know that may not have been your intention, and I'd love for us to discuss it."

Template 3: The "Ownership and Repair" Approach

Use when you're the one who made a mistake and want to restore trust.

"I've realized that [action or inaction] may have affected you negatively, and I want to take full responsibility for that. I'm truly sorry and want to know how I can help repair any impact this may have had on our trust."

Pro Tip: Always end with a question that invites healing:

- "How did that experience land with you?"
- "What would help rebuild trust moving forward?"
- "What can I do differently next time?"

Team Trust Rebuilding Worksheet

Use after a season of disconnection, leadership change, layoffs, or conflict.

Instructions: Give this worksheet to each team member (anonymous or named) and use it to foster healing dialogue in a group debrief or 1-on-1s.

Section 1: Reflecting on the Past
- What recent situations or seasons have impacted my ability to trust the team or leadership?
- When did I feel most disconnected or discouraged?
- What happened?

Section 2: Honoring What's Working
- What is one thing our team does well when it comes to collaboration or support?
- Who has consistently demonstrated trustworthiness, and how?

Section 3: Moving Toward Repair
- What specific behaviors or actions would help rebuild my trust in the team?
- What would make me feel safe, seen, and supported moving forward?

Section 4: My Ownership
- What is one way I can take responsibility for re-building trust on this team?
- What small step am I willing to take this week to contribute to healing?

Shared Team Journaling Prompts for Restoration

Use in meetings, retreats, or team reflection spaces. Ideal for printing or sharing digitally.

Instructions: Have each team member write a brief response to one or more prompts. Then invite voluntary sharing, or gather responses for themes and insights.

- "One thing I appreciate about this team is…"
- "Something I hope we grow stronger in together is…"
- "I feel most energized at work when…"
- "A time I felt truly supported here was…"
- "If I could speak honestly (without fear), I'd say…"
- "One act of kindness I'll commit to this week is…"
- "The culture I'd love us to build is one where…"

Optional Integration Tip: Collect themes and turn them into a "Team Restoration Vision" that is printed, framed, or emailed to all participants.

CHAPTER 12: LEADERSHIP REIMAGINED: LOVE, COURAGE, AND INTEGRITY

Leadership Self-Reflection Inventory

A Weekly Heart Check for Leaders Who Want to Grow in Love, Courage, and Integrity

Use this inventory once a week (or monthly) to reflect on how well you are embodying restorative leadership. Be honest, not harsh. Growth begins with awareness.

Instructions: Rate each statement from 1–5
(1 = Rarely True, 5 = Consistently True)
Statement   Rating (1–5)

___I lead with compassion, not control.

___I actively listen without interrupting.

___I own my mistakes and apologize when needed.

___I prioritize people over tasks.

___I seek feedback regularly and respond without defensiveness.

___I speak life and encouragement into my team.

___I honor different perspectives, even when I disagree.

___I make time for my own rest, reflection, and spiritual renewal.

___I pray over my team and invite God into my leadership.

___I make decisions based on values, not just pressure.

Reflection Questions:

1. Where am I strongest as a restorative leader?
2. What's one area I want to intentionally grow in this week?
3. Who could support me in that growth?

Sample Team Discussion Guide: Reimagining Leadership Together

Ideal for a team retreat, leadership meeting, or book club discussion

Opening Prompt:

"Think of a leader who deeply impacted your life. What did they do that made you feel seen, safe, or supported?"

Key Discussion Questions:

1. What does outstanding leadership mean to you today, and how has that changed over time?
2. What do our current employees, students, or clients need most from us as leaders?
3. Where have we unintentionally led from fear or control instead of love and purpose?
4. What systems (meetings, evaluations, communication practices) reinforce old leadership models, and what could we redesign?
5. What are three words we want people to feel when they think of our leadership?

Action Step:

Each team member writes one "Leadership Commitment" on a sticky note or notecard (e.g., "I commit to listening with empathy this quarter" or "I commit to giving timely, kind feedback"). Place all the notes on a board or wall as your shared leadership vision.

Courageous Conversations Framework for Leaders

How to lead hard conversations with humility, clarity, and restoration in mind

Step 1: Pray and Prepare

Ask the Holy Spirit for wisdom, timing, and the right words.

Clarify the real issue:

- What happened?
- What impact did it have?
- What outcome do you hope for?

Step 2: Create a Safe Environment

Choose a private, calm space. Open with grace and the intent to restore, not to punish.

Example Opening:
"I want to have a conversation that may be uncomfortable, but I believe it's important for our growth and our relationship. My goal is not to criticize, but to clarify and work together toward healing."

Step 3: Share Honestly + Listen Fully

Use "**I**" language, not accusations.

- "I noticed…"
- "I felt…"
- "I want to understand…"

Then pause. Let the other person speak. Listen without interruption.

Step 4: Seek Resolution, Not Victory

Ask:
1. "How can we move forward in a way that feels honest and honoring?"
2. "What would healing look like for both of us?"

Step 5: End with Encouragement + Follow-Up

- ☐ Affirm any positive contributions or efforts.
- ☐ Clarify next steps or expectations.
- ☐ Set a check-in to revisit progress.

Closing Tip: Keep restoration, not just resolution, as your end goal. Even if the issue is difficult, the tone should always be "We're in this together."

CHAPTER 13: CULTIVATING BELONGING AND HONOR IN EVERY WORKPLACE

Belonging Culture Checklist

Use this to assess and elevate the culture of belonging in your workplace.

Leadership Practices:

- Leaders greet employees by name and regularly check in personally.
- Leadership encourages diverse voices to contribute

in meetings.

- Team members feel safe sharing concerns or ideas without fear of judgment or retribution.
- Employee feedback is not only welcomed but also acted upon.
- Leaders acknowledge cultural celebrations, personal milestones, and differences with honor.

Organizational Policies:

- Clear channels exist for reporting bias or discrimination.
- Wellness and mental health are treated as organizational priorities.
- Team rituals (e.g., gratitude circles, birthdays, shared wins) foster unity.
- Team-building activities are designed for inclusion, not just for extroverts or dominant voices.

Team Dynamics:

- No one consistently feels "othered" or left out of key conversations.
- Meetings include space for all roles, not just senior voices.
- Language used in communication is inclusive, transparent, and compassionate.
- Employees feel free to bring their full selves to work, including their faith, family values, and cultural backgrounds.

Reflection Prompt:

1. Which 2–3 items are you already doing well?

2. Which 1–2 would be most transformative if implemented in your organization this quarter?

Sample Employee Recognition Templates

Use these templates to regularly affirm team members in a way that reinforces value, identity, and impact.

1. Personalized Affirmation Note (Physical or Digital):

"Dear [Employee Name],

I just wanted to pause and say how much I appreciate your heart, consistency, and character. Your [specific contribution] made a huge impact this week. You bring more than skills; you bring strength and spirit. Thank you for being such a vital part of our team.

With gratitude,

[Your Name]"

2. Peer-to-Peer Shoutout Slack or Teams Message

"Can we all take a moment to celebrate [Name] today? The way they handled [brief story] was a beautiful example of compassion and leadership. So grateful you're on this team!"

3. Public Acknowledgement in Meetings:

"Before we move on, I want to spotlight [Name]. Even when things get tough, the integrity and joy you bring have not gone unnoticed. You are a gift to this workplace."

4. Team Recognition Board Prompt:

"Who on your team modeled honor, courage, or healing this week? Add a note to the Recognition Wall today."

Empowerment Tip: Make recognition a weekly rhythm, not a yearly review.

Belonging & Honor Leadership Reflection Guide

Use this personal reflection tool to check your own leadership lens and create space for honest growth.

Journal Prompts:

1. When was the last time I intentionally honored someone I disagree with?
2. Do all members of my team feel psychologically safe with me? How do I know?
3. How do I handle feedback from above, peers, and below?
4. Whose voice might I be unintentionally tuning out or overlooking?
5. Have I created space for cultural or spiritual expression in appropriate, honoring ways?
6. What systems or habits might be causing some team members to feel excluded?
7. Who have I seen grow this month, and have I told them?

Scripture Meditation:

Be devoted to one another in love. Honor one another above yourselves. — Romans 12:10, NIV

Empowerment Strategy: Set a recurring calendar reminder each month to sit with these prompts and make one meaningful adjustment to how you lead with honor and belonging.

CHAPTER 14: FROM WORKPLACE TO WORLD-CHANGER, HOW SMALL ACTS TRANSFORM CULTURES

Small Acts, Big Impact Challenge Guide

Transform your workplace culture one intentional act at a time.

Big change doesn't begin with big budgets. It begins with small, daily choices rooted in love, courage, and intention.

Use this 7-day challenge to jumpstart a culture of healing right where you are. Print it, share it with your team, or use it as a personal commitment.

Day 1: Speak Life
☐ Write and share a specific, heartfelt affirmation with one coworker.

Example: "I see how committed you are behind the scenes. Your excellence inspires me."

Day 2: Thank Unexpectedly
☐ Send a thank-you email or card to someone who rarely gets recognized: a janitor, admin, or IT person.
Bonus: Handwrite it!

Day 3: Listen Generously
☐ Give someone the gift of uninterrupted attention. Ask a genuine question and listen without interrupting.

Day 4: Ask to Understand
☐ Approach a team tension or disagreement with curiosity instead of defense. Ask: "Can you help me understand how you experienced that?"

Day 5: Celebrate a Small Win

☐ Publicly acknowledge a team or individual's success (no matter how small) in a meeting, chat, or email thread.

Day 6: Offer Support Without Being Asked

☐ Notice someone struggling, and step in. Offer help without waiting to be invited.

Day 7: Invite Belonging

☐ Invite someone who may feel overlooked to lunch, coffee, or a team brainstorm. Let them know they matter.

Remember: Culture changes one conversation at a time. Be the spark.

Daily World-Changer Reflection Journal

Shift your mindset. Cultivate healing. Create impact. Use this journaling framework daily or weekly to stay grounded in your workplace calling. Each prompt is designed to help you reflect, reset, and reignite your sense of purpose.

1. Today I showed up as a Restorer by…(What action or attitude reflected healing, honor, or hope?)

2. One person I encouraged or supported was…(How did you impact their day or perspective?)

3. A moment I'm grateful for today…(Even in tension, find the gold. Gratitude heals hearts.)

4. A challenge I faced… and how I responded…(Did I choose peace? Did I need a reset? What will I do differ-

ently?)

5. One step I will take tomorrow to bring healing to my workplace is...(Make it small. Make it specific. Make it sacred.)

Declaration

Write your own or repeat: "I am a Restorer. I carry healing in my heart, hope in my voice, and purpose in my hands. Today, I made a difference."

Personal Destiny Activation Checklist

Ready to walk boldly in your God-given assignment at work? Use this checklist to activate your next level of destiny.

☐ I have written a clear Workplace Mission Statement that reflects my purpose.

☐ I speak life-giving words to others and myself regularly.

☐ I take time daily to pray over my workplace, team, and leadership.

☐ I have a clear plan for weekly emotional, spiritual, and physical renewal.

☐ I actively seek opportunities to grow, even when they feel uncomfortable.

☐ I practice accountability and seek feedback regularly.

☐ I choose to heal, not hide, when tension or conflict arises.

☐ I know my gifts, and I use them boldly and humbly.

☐ I recognize that I am part of something bigger, a

movement of restoration.

☐ I mentor, encourage, or lift someone else weekly, because destiny is never just about me.

☐ I reflect weekly on where God is moving in my workplace and how I can partner with Him.

☐ I see my workplace as a sacred space for purpose, transformation, and legacy.

Reflection Prompt:

What is one area I need to recommit to this week to walk fully in my workplace destiny?

CHAPTER 15: DESIGNING ORGANIZATIONS THAT HEAL AND PROSPER

Healing Workplace Design Checklist

Designing a culture where people thrive, not just survive. Use this checklist to evaluate and improve the healing potential of your workplace:

Leadership Practices:
- Leaders model vulnerability, empathy, and emotional intelligence.
- Leaders practice and encourage healthy boundaries.
- Senior leaders demonstrate humility and accountability.

Culture & Communication:
- Open-door policy for safe, judgment-free conversations.
- Recognition programs celebrate not just results, but

values and growth.
- Conflicts are resolved respectfully and promptly.

Team Support & Belonging:
- Personal milestones (birthdays, family news, wellness wins) are celebrated.
- Team-building and restorative activities are offered regularly.

Wellness & Flexibility:
- Flexible scheduling or remote options are available where possible.
- Employees are encouraged to take breaks, vacations, and mental health days.
- Quiet spaces are available for reflection, prayer, or rest.

Spiritual & Emotional Health:
- Optional prayer groups or spiritual encouragement resources exist.
- Counseling or coaching support is accessible and de-stigmatized.
- Teams are equipped to discuss emotional wellness openly.

Growth & Empowerment:
- Employees have access to personal/professional development resources.
- Mentorship and leadership pipelines are active and inclusive.
- Employees are empowered to lead initiatives and express new ideas.

Next Step:
☐ Review this list with your leadership team.
☐ Identify 2–3 priority areas to improve within 90 days.
☐ Reassess each quarter to track healing progress.

Sample Ethical Leadership Commitment Templates

Because ethics and empathy must lead together.

Option 1: Personal Commitment Statement (For Leaders)

As a leader in this organization, I commit to leading with integrity, transparency, and humility.

I will speak the truth even when it costs, listen with the intent to understand, and treat all team members with equal dignity. I will be accountable to this company's values, model healthy boundaries, and pursue justice, not favoritism. I believe leadership is stewardship.

I am not just managing tasks; I am shaping lives.

Option 2: Team Agreement for Ethical Culture (For Group Signatures)

We, the leadership team of [Organization Name], agree to:
- Uphold truth and transparency in all communications.
- Protect confidentiality while honoring accountability.
- Create space for feedback without fear of retaliation.
- Address ethical concerns swiftly and compassionately.

- Model work-life balance and mental wellness practices.
- Honor each person's dignity regardless of role, background, or belief.

Signed by: _____
(Include space for each signee's name, role, and date.)

Usage Tip: Print and frame these in leadership offices or display them in team rooms to create accountability and cultural visibility.

Wellness Program Launch Guide

A restorative workplace starts with strategic, supportive wellness programs.

Assess Employee Needs

Distribute a short anonymous survey to assess:

- Stress levels
- Mental/emotional wellness interest
- Fitness/nutrition goals
- Preferred wellness formats (workshops, self-paced, challenges)

Build Your Wellness Dream Team

☐ Appoint a cross-functional "Wellness Committee" of 3–5 champions.
☐ Include HR, a representative from leadership, and diverse employees.

Set Program Goals & Budget

Examples of measurable goals:
- Reduce burnout by 25% in 6 months
- Improve engagement scores by 15%

Launch monthly wellness workshops or quiet room access. Suggested budget: $50–$100 per employee annually to start

Design & Launch the Core Elements

Wellness Elements Can Include:

- Emotional: Resilience or mindfulness workshops
- Physical: Group walking challenges or fitness classes
- Spiritual: Optional prayer groups or quiet spaces
- Relational: Monthly "connect + coffee" events
- Mental: Therapy stipends or access to online counseling apps

Kickoff Event Ideas:

- "Wellness Week" with free daily activities and prizes
- Guest speakers (faith leaders, mental health professionals)
- Gift employees with wellness planners or journals
- Promote + Normalize
- Incorporate wellness into staff meetings and leadership messages.
- Share stories/testimonials to make wellness visible and valued.
- Train managers to champion, not compete with, work-life wellness.

Review & Adjust Quarterly

- ☐ Collect data: attendance, feedback, testimonials
- ☐ Reassess needs and pivot with purpose

CHAPTER 16: YOUR DESTINY AWAITS, THE WORKPLACE RESTORATION MOVEMENT STARTS WITH YOU

Workplace Restorer's Manifesto Template

A personal commitment to build, heal, and lead with love and integrity.

Instructions: Read this manifesto aloud. Sign it, date it, and post it somewhere visible to remind yourself daily of the calling you carry.

I Am a Workplace Restorer:

- I am called to cultivate healing, unity, and purpose in every room I enter.
- I believe that the workplace can be a sanctuary for growth, wholeness, and God-given destiny.
- I commit to lead with integrity, even when it's hard.
- To choose grace over gossip.
- To speak life in rooms filled with discouragement.
- To forgive quickly, communicate clearly, and hold others with compassion.
- I will build bridges, not walls.
- I will model empathy, not ego.
- I will be a safe place, a well-watered garden, for those around me
- I believe healing is holy.

APPENDIX A

- Honor is powerful.
- And restoration is possible.
- I was born for such a time as this, and I accept the assignment.

Signed: _____

Date: _____

Small Acts of Restoration Challenge List

Because revival doesn't start with a policy; it starts with one person, you.

Use this *21-Day Challenge* to bring light, kindness, and healing energy into your workplace culture. These simple actions, when done with love and consistency, change everything. Try it. Let's just see what happens.

Day 1: Write a thank-you note to someone who has gone unseen.

Day 2: Start your next meeting with a moment of gratitude or reflection.

Day 3: Encourage someone publicly in front of others.

Day 4: Offer to help a team member complete a project or task.

Day 5: Forgive someone quietly, even if they don't apologize.

Day 6: Post a positive quote or scripture at your workstation.

Day 7: Ask someone how they're really doing. Then listen.

Day 8: Share a personal story of growth or resilience to inspire your team.

Day 9: Pray for your workplace during your commute.

Day 10: Refuse to engage in gossip. Walk away with

grace.

Day 11: Bring in snacks, flowers, or a treat "just because."

Day 12: Invite someone new to lunch or coffee.

Day 13: Create a "Kindness Wall" or "Gratitude Board."

Day 14: Suggest a moment of silence or prayer before a big meeting.

Day 15: Send an uplifting email or message to the entire team.

Day 16: Ask a leader how you can support their vision.

Day 17: Recommend a wellness resource (counselor, coach, book).

Day 18: Highlight someone's contribution who is often overlooked.

Day 19: Reflect on one thing YOU need to heal, and take one step.

Day 20: Speak up in a moment of injustice with grace and courage.

Day 21: Celebrate someone else's success as if it were your own.

Bonus: Share your story after 21 days. What changed in you? What changed around you?

Personal Healing Growth Tracker

Because transformation is both spiritual and strategic. Use this tracker weekly (or monthly) to reflect on your journey as a Workplace Restorer. Healing happens in layers, and this tool helps you honor every step.

Week/Month: _____

1. How did I intentionally show up as a Restorer this week?

- ☐ Encouraged someone
- ☐ Defused conflict
- ☐ Practiced active listening
- ☐ Modeled vulnerability
- ☐ Set healthy boundaries
- ☐ Offered forgiveness
- ☐ Elevated someone's voice
- ☐ Protected my peace
- ☐ Prayed over my workplace
- ☐ Spoke life instead of criticism
- ☐ Led with empathy
- ☐ Celebrated a team member
- ☐ Created space for others to heal

2. What challenged me this week, and how did I respond?

(Reflect in 2–3 sentences or bullet points.)

3. Where did I experience growth, healing, or a mindset shift?

4. What lesson did the Holy Spirit teach me this week?

5. What's one restoration goal for next week?

Affirmation of the Week:

"Through Christ, I bring light, healing, and peace to every space I enter."

Marla A. McCarthy is a passionate workplace transformer, empowerment coach, and sought-after speaker who believes that healing hearts transforms companies and destinies. With a unique blend of spiritual insight, leadership experience, and real-world compassion, Marla equips leaders, employees, and organizations to break cycles of burnout, restore broken relationships, and cultivate cultures of honor, healing, and high performance.

A mother of seven, wife, coach, and faith-filled strategist, Marla understands the pressures of balancing business with purpose. Her voice resonates across boardrooms and breakrooms alike, offering timeless wisdom and practical tools that bridge the gap between productivity and people, metrics and mission. She helps leaders and team members in workplaces to rediscover what matters most: *the value of every person and the power of unity.*

Through her coaching, books, and speaking engagements, Marla has helped numerous people begin the courageous journey toward emotional health, relational trust, and restorative leadership. She doesn't just talk about transformation and restoration, she lives it, and she equips others to do the same.

Whether you're a CEO, team leader, HR director, or a staff member hungry for change, Marla invites you to view your workplace as more than just a job. It's a place to fulfill your purpose, it's your Kingdom assignment, and healing it might just be the key to unlocking the destiny you've been praying for.

ISBN: 979-8-9989754-6-2

www.ingramcontent.com/pod-product-compliance
Lightning Source LLC
Chambersburg PA
CBHW021705120626
46545CB00004B/1418